Bridging the silos

Enterprise-architecture for IT-architects

Tom Graves

Tetradian Consulting

Published by
Tetradian Books
Unit 215, Communications House
9 St Johns Street, Colchester, Essex CO2 7NN
England

http://www.tetradianbooks.com

First published December 2008
ISBN 978-1-906681-02-9 (paperback)
ISBN 978-1-906681-03-6 (e-book)

Contents

An introduction...1

Basics – what is enterprise architecture? 4

Basics – the architecture process......................................13

Basics – artefacts and toolsets 17

Purpose – an overview...21

Purpose – business-driven architecture...........................29

Governance – an overview 35

Governance – roles and responsibilities 41

Governance – products 48

Framework – an overview..53

Framework – layers..59

Framework – primitives 63

Framework – composites..79

Framework – models..88

Framework – integration 97

Methodology – an overview 106

Methodology – preparation 113

Methodology – assessment...121

Methodology – solutions 146

Methodology – hands-off architecture 161

Completion – an overview 166

Completion – architecture artefacts 169

Completion – closing the loop 184

Glossary 193

Acknowledgements

By its nature as a 'conversion course' for IT-architects, this book draws extensively on existing frameworks and methodologies in common use in the IT-architecture space – in particular the Zachman Framework, and the Architecture Design Method (ADM) of The Open Group Architecture Framework (TOGAF). The author acknowledges that the originals are and remain the copyright of the Zachman Institute for Framework Advancement and The Open Group respectively. The adaptations described in this book were created in good faith to cover the needs of a broader purpose and broader market, and should not be interpreted as making any claims as to ownership of the original work.

Amongst others, the following people kindly provided comments and feedback on the various drafts of this book: Daljit Banger (White Knight Consulting, GB), Sally Bean (London, GB), Charles Edwards (ProcessWave, GB), Michael Ellyett (RHE, NZ), Nigel Green (CapGemini, GB), Ziggy Jaworowski (NSW DoCS, Aus), Kim Parker (Australia Post, Aus), Liz Poraj-Wilczynska (Brockhampton, GB), Marlies van Steenbergen (Sogeti, NL), Peter Tseglakof (Australia Post, Aus), Jaco Vermeulen (Orbital VX, GB). In particular, Michael Ellyett provided the innovative concept of 'hands-off architecture'.

Please note that, to preserve commercial and personal confidentiality, the stories and examples in this book have been adapted, combined and in part fictionalised from experiences in a variety of contexts, and do not and are not intended to represent any specific individual or organisation.

Registered trademarks such as Zachman, TOGAF, FEAF, ITIL, Macintosh etc are acknowledged as the intellectual property of the respective owners.

AN INTRODUCTION

An architecture for the enterprise

This book is about enterprise-architecture: not just IT-architecture, but *real* enterprise-architecture – the architecture of the enterprise as a whole.

Standard 'enterprise-architecture' descriptions, such as Zachman, TOGAF or FEAF (see *Resources* below), tend to imply that architecture begins and ends with IT. But IT architecture is just one part of a real enterprise-wide architecture, one subset of a much larger picture. Above all, the architecture needs to be *business-driven*, not technology-driven: the moment we forget that, we're in trouble straight away.

We need to remember, too, that there's a lot more to *real* IT than just 'computers and stuff'. A pencil is information technology; a whiteboard is information technology; likewise the humble sticky-note. Creating conditions for meaningful knowledge sharing is information technology – so the layout of the office café can be a crucial part of an organisation's information technology. I'd doubt if any of those items would rate even a single mention in your existing 'IT-systems' models – yet they're all essential aspects of a complete enterprise-architecture.

So the bad news is that real enterprise-architecture requires us to deal with a much broader scope than the familiar comfort-zone of IT-architecture. We *do* need our architecture to address that full scope – the entire enterprise – if we're to create viable solutions that bridge across all of the silos.

The good news, though, is that as an IT-architect you're already well-equipped to tackle this:

- you're a generalist, used to looking at things from multiple perspectives
- you know how to build models at different levels, from abstract, or conceptual, to logical, physical and operational
- you know how to use models to explain complex concepts to many different audiences, from board-level to operations staff
- you know how to derive models from real 'as-is' situations

- you know how to model an architecture from a strategy or a required 'to-be' scenario for a system's future
- you know how to derive practical solutions from abstract models

All the essential skills you'll need, in fact. All that you'll need to add is a stronger grasp of the much broader scope of architecture at a true *enterprise*-wide level, and a willingness to place IT into a more realistic role and perspective within the enterprise.

That's what this book is about.

What's in this book?

In the previous book in this series, *Real Enterprise-Architecture*, I described a systematic model and methodology for enterprise-level architecture, based on the classic Group Dynamics five-phase model of the project life-cycle. But it seems in practice it can feel too abstract at first, especially for IT solution-architects: it can be too much of a jump to go direct to that level.

So this book provides a 'conversion course' for IT-architects. It uses the same overall model as the previous book, with the same five phases or strands of the architecture process: but here the description for each strand is adapted from themes familiar to most IT-architects, such as Zachman, TOGAF, FEAF, ITIL, Agile, MSP and PRINCE2. The basic sequence is as follows:

- *Purpose* (see *Purpose – an overview*, p.21) – identifying the **business-purpose** of each architecture-iteration and the whole architecture – adapted from Agile, MSP and TOGAF
- *People* (see *Governance – an overview*, p. 35) – **governance** principles, responsibilities and procedures – adapted from MSP, PRINCE2 and TOGAF
- *Preparation* (see *Framework – an overview*, p. 53) – the **frameworks** used to keep architectural assessment information in context – adapted from Zachman and TOGAF
- *Process* (see *Methodology – an overview*, p.106) – the **methodology** for architecture assessment, solution-design and solution-implementation – adapted from TOGAF and Agile
- *Performance* (see *Completion – an overview*, p. 166) – the metrics and 'lessons-learned' processes used for **completion** and 'closing the loop' of the architecture cycle – adapted from TOGAF and PRINCE2.

Each section is split into bite-size chunks to apply straight away in your day-to-day work. Although there's a fair amount of theory, the keyword here is *practice*: the aim is to give you something that you can *use*. So each chapter includes examples and stories to place the ideas into a real-life context, with references to other relevant resources. There's also a glossary at the end of the book, which should help in clarifying the broader meaning of some of the common terms used in whole-of-enterprise architecture.

But before we explore that sequence, we first need to address some basic issues, such as identifying what we mean by 'enterprise architecture'. So that's where we'll start in the next chapter.

Resources

 Whole-of-enterprise architecture: see Tom Graves, *Real Enterprise Architecture: beyond IT to the whole enterprise*, (Tetradian, 2008)

 TOGAF (The Open Group Architecture Framework): see www.opengroup.org/togaf

 FEAF (Federal Enterprise Architecture Framework): see www.gao.gov/special.pubs/eaguide.pdf [PDF]

 Zachman framework: see www.zifa.org

 PRINCE2 (PRojects IN Controlled Environments): see www.www.prince2.org.uk

 ITIL (Information Technology Infrastructure Library): see www.itil.org.uk

 MSP (Managing Successful Programmes): see www.programmes.org

 Agile software / system development: see www.agilealliance.org and agilemanifesto.org

BASICS – WHAT IS ENTERPRISE ARCHITECTURE?

Summary

Enterprise-architecture: just two words, but to make sense of whole-of-enterprise architecture we need to be clear what we mean by each, as well as what's meant by the term as a whole. We also need to face the sheer scope of whole-of-enterprise architecture.

Details

Defining the enterprise

What is an enterprise? The FEAF document *A Practical Guide to Federal Enterprise Architecture* describes it as follows:

> [An enterprise is] an organisation or cross-functional entity supporting a defined business scope and mission.

> An enterprise includes interdependent resources – people, organisations and technology – who must coordinate their functions and share information in support of a common mission or set of related missions.

So far so good, but note the booby-trap here: 'enterprise' is *not* the same as 'organisation'. The *Practical Guide* warns:

> …it must be understood that in many cases, the enterprise may transcend established organisational boundaries – e.g. trade, grant management, financial management, logistics.

Rather like the dreaded 'org-chart', the boundaries of the organisation tell us very little about the real bounds of the enterprise – the "defined business scope and mission". In practice, an enterprise is a *value-web* that includes the organisation's partners, suppliers, customers and all the other stakeholders within the scope of that 'mission', with structures and relationships that may well be changing dynamically from minute to minute.

Throw a few other factors into the mix – such as outsourced business-critical functions, continuous '24/7' processes, or 'follow-the-sun' operations with interfaces shared worldwide across an entire industry – and the old notion that the organisation *is* the enterprise will seem more like a charming relic of a bygone age.

That's problematic enough in itself. But where it gets *really* messy is governance (see *Governance – an overview*, p.35). If the enterprise is more than the organisation, where are the boundaries of governance? Whose rules apply, and in which contexts? More on that later when we look at frameworks and governance.

Defining architecture

To understand architecture, let's look at the definition from the *Practical Guide*:

> [Architecture is] the structure of components, their interrelationships, and the principles and guidelines governing their evolution and design.

It's a good definition, though in some ways more for what it *doesn't* say than for what it does. It doesn't specify 'information technology', it says "components [and] their interrelationships" – leaving the definition open for the broader interpretation we're going to need.

But this still doesn't say much about the *nature* of that structure, and its "evolution and design". Most IT architecture is like the design of a single building: we describe the present state of the building, then what we want it to look like – the so-called 'future-state' – and some kind of plan or 'roadmap' to get from here to there. But at the enterprise level, architectural design is closer to town planning, or even the structure of an entire city. And at this level, it's orders of magnitude more complex. The world is not static, but emergent, unfolding; there *is* no identifiable 'future-state'. We still need vision, a sense of future – or future*s*, plural – but we need to work with something a great deal more flexible and fluid than a single, simple 'plan'.

Defining enterprise-architecture

To put this together, probably the best starting-point for a definition of enterprise-architecture comes from the Wikipedia:

> Enterprise Architecture is the description of the current and/or future structure and behaviour of an organisation's processes, information systems, personnel and organisational sub-units, aligned with the organisation's core goals and strategic direction.

The FEAF *Practical Guide* refers to this "description" as a 'strategic information asset-base'. But unlike the *Practical Guide*, the Wikipedia article also adds a crucial rider on scope:

> Although often associated strictly with information technology, [EA] relates more broadly to the practice of business optimisation in that it addresses business architecture, performance management, organisational structure and process architecture as well.

A much broader scope, explicitly aligned to a core *business*-question. When properly implemented, the 'strategic information asset-base' that EA manages is best described as 'the enterprise's knowledge of itself'. So let's use that as working definition:

Enterprise-architecture is a discipline through which an enterprise can identify, develop and manage its knowledge of its purpose, its structure and itself.

The business-*purpose* of that managed knowledge is to support organisational and enterprise change – what the enterprise is and does, where it's going, its choices in that journey. This suggests, in turn, that the business role for the EA unit would be as a support for an enterprise-wide programme-management office (PMO) – providing information about the constantly-changing form of the enterprise, and guiding ideas and strategies about the best use of the enterprise's resources.

But because, wrongly, EA is often "associated strictly with information technology", the usual place we find an EA unit is as a subset of IT governance – which is *not* a good idea. To understand why, we need to look at little more closely at the impact of scope.

Scope and enterprise-architecture

The real concern with scope is this: are we thinking wide enough to cover what the context actually *needs*? If we're not careful about our assumptions, things can go spectacularly wrong – yet because our assumptions prevent us from seeing what's happening, we become incapable of understanding *why* things are going wrong. If we don't have a wide enough scope, we'll pour more and more resources into the only part of the problem we can see – but things just keep on getting worse, and we can't see why, or how.

> Sometimes even the most basic of reality-checks can get lost along the way. A real conversation from a Denver-Boston flight, way too many years ago.
>
> "I'm a senior project leader on Strategic Defense Initiative", he'd said, with patriotic pride. "You know – our space-based anti-missile shield!"

> I'll admit I stifled a bleak laugh. "How does it work?" I asked.
>
> "It fires an X-ray laser at the target – using a nuclear bomb inside itself to generate the laser."
>
> "A nuclear bomb? In space? Isn't that in breach of international treaty?"
>
> "No-one cares about *that*", he said, airily: no further questions there...
>
> "So, uh, how does it defend itself against possible attack?"
>
> "It fires off the X-ray laser, of course." Scornful.
>
> "I don't get it", I said. "Doesn't that mean its only defence – even against a dummy missile – is to blow itself up?"
>
> Sudden silence. A long pause. "We hadn't thought of that", he said...

Far, far too often, the technology comes first, and middle and last as well. The scope ends up being defined back-to-front, with the core business-needs all but forgotten. In one of my recent projects, for example, the IT group demanded that the business should redesign all its processes to fit in with the limitations of their badly-botched CRM implementation. In the project before that, the team-lead insisted that his made-up UML use-cases *were* the business-requirements – he'd never bothered to ask the business what they wanted. As an enterprise-architect, I must admit I'm a bit fed up of having to sort out the resultant mess.

The painful fact is that whenever technology takes the front seat, we end up with an expensive mess that doesn't *quite* do what's needed and has subtle yet serious side-effects. For which the only solution offered is yet another inadequately-thought-through technological 'fix', which also doesn't solve any actual problem but costs yet another lost fortune. And all too often, IT-centric 'enterprise architecture' has been just one more example: round and round on the same horrendously expensive cycle, getting nowhere faster and faster...

So the key concerns about scope are these:

- when dealing with any real-world issue, any restriction on scope and 'solutions' will always cause *big* problems
- it's all too easy to artificially restrict scope by staying within our comfort-zone – sticking to what we 'know', to what we think we're certain of, to what we can control
- with a narrow focus, we have no means to see *why* things are failing – and we make things worse by trying to force things to fit our too-limited assumptions

To avoid classic IT-centric disasters, we need to keep challenging our assumptions about scope. Which is rarely easy or comfortable, but we *must* do so, because in the real world, every item is connected to everything else in some sense or other. Any restrictions we place on scope are an operational convenience, not a 'fact'. So what we need to remember is this:

There's always another view, another way to do it.

And that other way may well be better – more efficient, more effective – than what we're doing now.

> I started my professional career as a typographer, moving sideways through computer-based typesetting to more mainstream IT. I was fortunate to work with some of the best consultants in pre-press, and one incident comes to mind here.
>
> At a directory-publishing operation, the programmers were building an application to go direct-to-plate from the mainframe database. They'd struggled for days with a peculiar one-off case that wrecked one section of output at the end of a very expensive thousand-page run. And there seemed to be no way to get the system to do it right.
>
> My colleague listened to all the lamentations, looked at the galley-prints on the cutting-board, and grinned. He reached into his briefcase, pulled out a scalpel, and with a few deft strokes re-arranged the offending symbols into the required order. The whole thing took a matter of seconds – and the result was exactly what was needed.
>
> The programmers looked on in horror. "We can't do that with code!", said one. "That's *cheating*!"
>
> "Cheating?" said the consultant, with a wry smile. "Getting the job out the door right, on time and on budget, is 'cheating'?" A few crestfallen faces; embarrassed shuffling of feet. "Getting the code right is important; but it's easy to forget the *why* for the code in the first place." He placed the scalpel on the desk. "Keep it", he said. "Label it 'for emergency use only', if you like – but there are times when it's the best tool we have!"

This is another reason why it's dangerous to place enterprise architecture under the 'IT governance' banner. Viewing the world through an IT-only lens means that, almost inevitably, we'll try to use IT methods to 'solve' problems for which IT isn't suited. To make sense of the whole, we need to start our overview from a much higher viewpoint than the detailed operations-level of one IT-centric subset in the enterprise – which is where we'd find conventional 'enterprise-architecture'. So we need to anchor our scope on one simple fact:

Every activity begins and ends with a business purpose.

No matter where we set our scope - even from right at the top of the enterprise – we'll still get lost if we lose sight of the 'why' of the enterprise. Without that anchor, the pressures of day to day business can push us a long way off track before we've had a chance to notice it – and once we do become aware of what's happened, it can take a long time get back on track. Even in the fine detail of moment-to-moment operations, we need some way to keep track of the business-purpose of what we're doing.

A painful personal example. As a writer and typographer, I moved into typesetting to gain more control over the production of my books. But I got sidetracked into running a typesetting business, to pay for the typesetting-system; and thence into micro-computers, to get more value out of our machines and make them more available to others.

Like so many people, I got hooked on code – that ever-elusive goal of getting the wretched machine to do what I *wanted* it to do! Hence rather too many all-night sessions, coding and debugging and the like – all of it in low-level assembly-language, in those days. Not far off a coffee-addiction. And *way* too much stress all round.

A year or so later, I was running what had become probably the first real microcomputer-based desktop-publishing operation in Britain – half a decade before the Macintosh and PageMaker. We wrote code to typeset magazines, partworks, bank rates-tables, even crossword-puzzles. A tiny operation, based in the back end of Britain, doing innovative, world-leading work for some of the largest companies in the country. It was a heady time.

But what I *didn't* do was write books. I'd lost track of the original business-purpose.

It wasn't till some years later, sifting through the metaphoric wreckage of what had once been my own company, that I realised what I'd done, and what I'd lost. Others had long since taken over in my previous profession: it was way too late to go back. All I could do was go forward, to start again in another field of interest – and keep reminding myself to remember the real business-purpose in whatever I did.

The inverse is also true: if we're starting from the high-level 'helicopter view' of strategy and the like, we have to remind ourselves of what's happening and what it's like right down in the low-level detail of operations. It's all the same continuum – the same body of knowledge, 'the enterprise's knowledge of itself' – that architecture needs to manage on behalf of the whole enterprise.

That's where IT-architects have a great advantage. Unlike most strategy-folks at one end of that continuum, and most operations-folks at the other, we're used to dealing with entities at every level. But whilst we're likely to be good at managing depth, as IT-architects what we're *not* likely to be good at as yet is breadth: a broad enough grasp of the *whole* of the enterprise, in all its complexity. So that key difference between *IT*-architecture and real *enterprise* architecture is what we need to turn to next.

Broadening the scope

In conventional IT-centric architecture, the world of the enterprise is divided up into four neat packages – business, data, applications, and technology – organised into a neat vertical hierarchy. For a top-down view of the enterprise, we start from 'business' and strategy; for a bottom-up view we start from the low-level details of technology.

There are a few variations: TOGAF's hierarchy is as above, whilst FEAF places applications above data, and others add an extra 'information' layer between 'business' and 'data'. But in essence this, we're told, is the complete scope of enterprise architecture – all that we need to work with, all that we need to know:

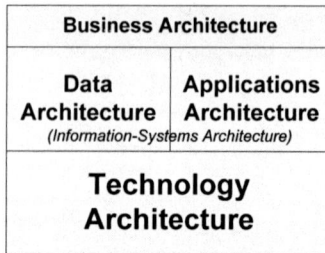

Business Architecture	
Data Architecture	Applications Architecture
(Information-Systems Architecture)	
Technology Architecture	

The IT-architecture hierarchy

Which is, bluntly, just plain stupid. To ask one really simple question, where do people fit within this scheme of things? Nowhere, is the short answer. Yet ITIL, the most commonly-used IT service management framework, insists that people are at the core of all service-management issues. Even from an IT perspective this 'standard' hierarchy is too incomplete to be any real use. So what's gone wrong? And what can we do about it?

The problem stems from enterprise-architecture's history. It began with piecemeal attempts to rein in some of the more rampant computer-based chaos, and later gained an expanding breadth of coverage as people started to realise that everything was dependent on everything else. Eventually it became clear that this 'IT-architecture' needed an enterprise-wide scope – at which point some idiot started calling it 'enterprise-architecture', as a shorthand for 'enterprise-wide IT-architecture' But it's misleading, because *the focus is on the technology, not the enterprise.*

It's true there's an increasing awareness that IT-strategy needs to be business-driven: but in most cases 'business-architecture' is just a label for 'everything not-IT', a kind of random grab-bag with low-level business-processes all jumbled together with high-level business strategy and everything in between. And it's still so technology-centric that the TOGAF Enterprise Edition methodology, for example, assigns more than six times the number of assessment-steps to technology than to all the rest of the business.

In short, it's not *enterprise*-architecture at all: it's an IT-centred mess. TOGAF gives us its fixed hierarchy of business, data, applications and systems-technology; but the *real* world includes people, and the knowledge held in people's heads, and cars and trucks and printing-presses and fork-lift-trucks and other machines that don't have a scrap of IT in them, and a great deal more besides. In other words, a *real* enterprise architecture needs to describe a world that looks more like this:

Purpose (Aspirational dimension) Business Architecture		IT domain (typical)
People Systems-Architecture	Information/Knowledge Systems-Architecture	Machine / Asset Systems-Architecture
Manual-Process Detail-Architecture	Information-Process Detail-Architecture	Machine-Process Detail-Architecture (Technology Architecture)
People (Relational dimension)	Knowledge (Conceptual dimension)	Assets / 'Things' (Physical dimension)

A more realistic hierarchy for TOGAF

Another way to portray this is to show the major dimensions – purpose, relations, knowledge and physical 'things' – as axes in a tetrahedral relationship.

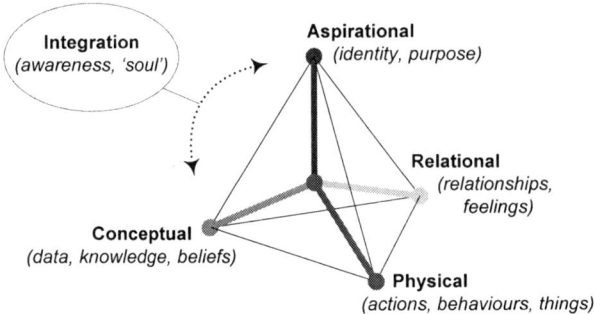

The tetradian: rotating the hierarchy

Rotating attention between each axis of this *tetradian* helps to keep the perspective in balance: This is true even for an IT-centric organisation such as a bank or an insurance firm; far more so for manufacturers and retailers and others, such as most government departments, for whom IT is simply an enabler, not the core of the business.

An IT-centric view of the enterprise, TOGAF-style, is simply one possible *view* into the broader scope represented by the whole enterprise. But it's only one of *many* possible views, all of them equally valid. So please, let's hammer this point home:

Enterprise architecture covers the whole enterprise

IT is one small subset of the enterprise

IT-architecture is one small subset of enterprise-architecture

Because as enterprise-architects, if we ever forget that, we're in deep trouble.

Application

- What is your current definition of 'enterprise architecture'?
- What is the current scope of the enterprise?
- What is the current scope of enterprise-architecture?
- Where – if at all – is enterprise-architecture sited in your organisation?

Resources

- FEAF: *A Practical Guide to Federal Enterprise Architecture*: see www.gao.gov/special.pubs/eaguide.pdf [PDF]
- ITIL: see www.itil-officialsite.com
- TOGAF layers: see www.opengroup.org/architecture/togaf8-doc/arch/toc.html (chapter 'TOGAF as an Enterprise Architecture Framework')
- Wikipedia summary on enterprise-architecture: see en.wikipedia.org/wiki/Enterprise_architecture

BASICS – THE ARCHITECTURE PROCESS

Summary

The architecture process has two distinct phases: assessment against requirements, in order to derive an overall design; and oversight of implementation, to ensure the final result does match both the design and the requirements. This applies to every level of structural change, from a single project to the whole enterprise. In whole-of-enterprise architecture, a key complication is that the world moves on whilst implementation takes place: design for flexibility is a must.

Details

In the physical world, the architecture discipline will design structures to serve a practical purpose. Enterprise-architecture does much the same for the practical purposes of the enterprise, though in a broader sense. Although building-design may well come into it at times, the 'structures' it designs are more likely to be of systems or workflows or aggregations of information. If a structure of *any* kind in the enterprise needs to change, enterprise-architecture should be involved.

In practice, the *process* of architecture is every bit as important as its visible outcomes. Conversations and dialogue between the various stakeholders about their architectural issues will matter as much as the designs and other end-products of that process, because it helps to build a more general awareness and under-standing of the enterprise *as a whole*, an interdependent 'system of systems'. This in itself should provide opportunities to enhance overall effectiveness in the enterprise.

Whatever the structure in question – whether an IT-network, a decision-tree, a work-breakdown structure, an assembly-line or any of an infinity of other combinations between physical, virtual, relational and other contexts – the architecture process usually has two distinct phases:

- *assessment* against requirements, comparing current context to desired future context(s) – see *Methodology – assessment*, p.121

13

- *solution design*, comparing desired requirements against real-world constraints, and deriving, designing and supervising implementation of appropriate solutions – see *Methodology – solutions*, p.146

A key distinction is between *primitives* and *composites* – see 'Primitives versus composites' in *Framework – an overview*, p.55. John Zachman – the originator of information-systems architecture – asserts that architecture depends on primitives, whilst successful solutions depend on skilful use of composites created from those primitives. The set of primitives is described by the underlying metamodel of the framework. At present, the sets of primitives in the frameworks supported in the common 'enterprise architecture' toolsets – see *Basics – artefacts and toolsets*, p.17 – are still mostly focussed on computer-based IT. This can be a problem, because we need a much broader set for the whole-of-enterprise scope of real enterprise architecture – see *Framework – primitives*, p.63 and *Framework – composites*, p.79.

Composites are 'complete' when they link together all of the required components – assets, functions, locations, capabilities, events, decisions and so on – into a single unified whole. This 'completeness' is essential at the operations level; but we also need to be able to split those composites apart in order to redesign anything. In essence, components and solutions are usable only to the extent that they're architecturally 'complete', but are *re*-usable to the extent that they're architecturally *in*complete. So in the *assessment* phase of architecture, the core stages in redesign are:

- split existing composites into their primitives
- derive higher-level abstracts from these low-level primitives
- identify desirable common traits, such as consistency
- use these traits to guide re-assembling of *partially*-complete composites as 'building blocks'

In *solution-design*, we bring the restructured composites closer to 'completeness' by linking the building-blocks together in appropriate ways, and translating the higher-level abstracts into concrete form for implementation. Whilst domain-architects work at the detail-level, the role of the enterprise architect in supporting solution-design is to maintain consistency across *all* domains, and to ensure clean transitions at domain-boundaries, such as handovers between manual and IT-based parts of business-processes.

The art here, both in architecture and in solution design, is in designing composites that are stable and reliable within themselves, but can be reconfigured quickly into new combinations that support enterprise agility. This is where concepts such as service-oriented architecture come to the fore: viewing an entire enterprise as a network of interdependent services can provide clarity in what can otherwise often seem to be overwhelming complexity.

Architecture does not exist on its own: it's part of a much broader process of business transformation, supporting change within the enterprise. IT-architecture is typically viewed solely as part of the IT domain, and under IT governance – itself often a contributing cause of the much-lamented 'business/IT divide', as inappropriate attempts are made to apply IT-governance 'over the border' into manual-process domains. But at the enterprise-architecture level, *enterprise* governance needs to apply: architecture needs to be viewed here as a support-function to an enterprise-wide programme management office or its equivalent.

The art of architecture is also one of continual trade-off between what is architecturally 'pure' – consistent, elegant, explicit, definable – and what is achievable in the real world. These trade-offs are necessarily dynamic: no matter how much we may wish for such, there is no such thing as a stable 'future state'. If we forget either of these points, we're in serious trouble.

> Obsessing about architectural 'purity' is one of the quickest ways to kill credibility, but it's a mistake I've seen architects make so many times it's not funny.
>
> In one particularly painful example, at a large telco, the lead architect habitually berated anyone who failed to conform with his fixed ideas about technical perfection. Unfortunately, he had the support of the CIO in this mad crusade, so it wasn't long before the business-folks learned to avoid any contact with architecture. We watched in dismay as he sabotaged all our attempts at enterprise-wide cohesion, and took the entire architecture discipline there on a slow spiral into angry irrelevance. Years later, they're still recovering from the resultant shambles in their systems.
>
> Oh well: goes with the nature of the trade, I guess. But we do need to watch out for that tendency, in ourselves as well. Constantly. Carefully. All the time.

To get this right, we need to model the constraints as much as the entities and the requirements. The constraints are *dynamic*, changing over time with each change in technology, capability, market, regulation and so on – in other words, each solution is dependent on the entire milieu of constraints and desires.

So a key part of architecture in a controlled environment revolves around management of 'dispensations' – see *Architecture Dispensation Statement*, p.177, and *Dispensations register*, p.181 – or what the DyA methodology calls 'Design without architecture'. Each dispensation is a permission granted to a project to implement a solution that does not conform with the architecture: the point here is that in each case this should be seen as *temporary*, arising from constraints that applied at that time, and should be resolved as soon as practicable to bring it into line with the desired architecture. Review of dispensations is a key part of the architecture process, and needs to occur throughout the architecture cycle.

A more extreme strategy is to take a 'hands-off' approach to architecture, working *with* the complexity rather than trying to control it. In effect, the architecture team pulls back to an 'observer' role, with more emphasis on assessment of information provided by projects – see *Architecture Description Statement*, p.176 – to identify places where small interventions could have greatest value – see *Methodology – hands-off architecture*, p.161. In general, it's a style which works best in a relatively mature architectural context, and may only be necessary in a multi-partner enterprise where governance is harder to enforce, but it's an approach that's well worth exploring as the architecture matures.

Application

- What is your understanding of the meaning and role of 'architecture' within the enterprise?
- What does an architect actually *do*? In particular, what does an *enterprise*-architect do?
- To you, and to your enterprise, what is the architecture process? What are its relations to other enterprise change-processes?
- If the present architecture, and present understanding of architecture, is essentially IT-centric or even IT-only, what would need to change to cover the broader scope of the entire enterprise?

Resources

- DyA (Dynamic Architecture): see eng.dya.info/Home/
- TOGAF (The Open Group Architecture Framework): see www.opengroup.org/togaf

BASICS – ARTEFACTS AND TOOLSETS

Summary

Creation and maintenance of documents, models and other arte-facts will form a key part of every architect's working life. You'll need an appropriate toolset with which to do this.

Details

The most visible parts of an architect's work are all the docu-ments, models and other artefacts created, referenced, updated and otherwise used throughout the process.

There are a lot of them: not just the visual models – which is what everyone sees and knows as 'architecture' – but all the documents and the like that come before and after them. It's useful to classify these under the major themes for the architecture process:

- *Purpose*: strategy documents; literature review; market review; business-intelligence; legislation and regulation; requirements and constraints; issues, risks and opportunities
- *Governance*: core principles; standards; governance protocols, processes and guidelines; roles, responsibilities and competencies
- *Framework*: metamodels; reference models; industry standards and technical standards; glossary and thesaurus
- *Methodology*: models, blueprints, assessments, solution-designs, migration-plans, implementation-plans and other products of architecture work; formal work-requests, end-of-phase reviews and other documents for management of the architecture-cycle
- *Completion*: 'lessons learned' reviews; statistics and other metrics; maturity-models and other performance-metrics

There'll be more detail later on individual artefacts or 'products' (see *Governance – products*, p.48, and *Completion – architecture artefacts*, p.169). For now, the main question is how do you *do* all this stuff? How do you create it, share it, maintain it, manage it?

In an ideal world, *all* of it should be handled by a purpose-built toolset, with a single consistent user-interface. In the real world, unfortunately, we're a long way from that ideal.

> Despite a great deal of marketing hype, none of the current toolsets come anywhere close to handling the real needs of whole-of-enterprise architecture. Several of the best-known are little better than glorified CASE tools for software development, and so IT-centric that they can be more of a hindrance than a help. The tools that are based on metamodel repositories cover more of the scope, but tend to be hard to use and even harder to explain. A few tools do provide a small modicum of automated support for methodology and governance; one or two do a reasonable attempt to cope with the complexity of dynamic, versioned requirements; but at present none at all seem to include any means to handle issue-management or risk-management in an integrated manner.
>
> In short, the EA toolset scene is still a mess. Oh well.

So for the most part we're left to muddle along as best we can. For a simple setup such as a *small enterprise* or an experimental 'skunk-works', you're almost better off working on paper or a recording whiteboard. You don't need a toolset as such: what you really need is some means to support the *social* aspect of business-knowledge, sharing the awareness of the desired architecture through personal experience rather than through formal models. If you have one, you can use an 'agile development' toolset or an online-collaboration tool such as a wiki to manage some of the information on requirements, issues and risks. But the key point here is that everything to do with purpose, governance, framework, methodology and completion still needs to happen: but it happens most in people's heads and people's conversations.

For *pilot projects* in a *mid-sized enterprise*, it's possible – just – to get by for a while with office drawing-programs such as Visio for modelling, and simple spreadsheets for the data-storage and data-tracking. The catch is that simplicity and ease of use are traded off against concerns that rapidly become more and more important as scope and scale increase: live collaboration, versioning, access-control and, especially, linking between models, model-entities and requirements. For sanity's sake, you *must* support these with a formal requirements management process such as Volere (see *Resources* below), and some kind of disciplined issue-tracking and risk-tracking, either with spreadsheets, or preferably a purpose-built tool – a quick web-search will locate any number of low-cost or no-cost packages for this. You'll also need broader collaboration support, which usually means tackling the joyous politics of setting up your own intranet-servers and suchlike – but it does all have to be done at some point, so even for a pilot-project it's well worth doing now.

For whole-of-enterprise architecture in a *large enterprise*, don't even *think* of trying to do the work without proper toolset support. Struggling with the limitations of the present generation of toolsets is often an exercise in extreme frustration, but the sheer complexity is such that trying to do it with anything less would drive you mad in a matter of weeks. The full set of requirements for whole-of-enterprise architecture will depend on your specific needs, but you'll need the toolset to cover most of the following:

- a good range of built-in frameworks and model-types, covering all context layers (see *Framework – layers*, p.59), architectural 'primitives' (see *Framework – primitives*, p.63) and appropriate architecture 'composites' for your industry (see *Framework – composites*, p.79), sufficient to describe the full range of business-issues you'll need to address (see *Purpose – business-driven architecture*, p.29)

- good support for metamodelling, to create additional entity-types and model-types that you'll need for your own specific context

- graphical modelling – because most people find diagrams and drawings easier to understand than tables and plain text

- strong cross-referencing and cross-linking, not only between models, but between entities and the responsible stakeholders, and to the respective issues, risks, requirements and project-management 'gateways'

- strong versioning, sufficient to handle an almost infinitely complex mix of scenarios and status-types (potential, planned, scheduled, pilot, staging, implemented, production, sunset, decommission and many others)

- strong integrated support for appropriate governance (see *Governance – an overview*, p.35) and related portfolio- and programme-management methodologies (see *Methodology – an overview*, p.106), supported either by built-in scheduling and sequencing, or strong links to external project-management tools

- strong integrated support for management of requirements, issues, risks, opportunities and suchlike

- strong support for integrated standards, including enforcement of naming-standards, and a shared glossary and thesaurus

- strong integrated support for dynamic, versioned links to other enterprise-wide repositories for document-management and knowledge-sharing
- good web-based publishing facilities with two-way feedback, to allow stakeholders to comment and to advise of changes to architectural entities and models impacting their scope
- a versatile system for access-control, supporting any required combination of 'need to know, need to use'

There's a lot of functionality in that list, so don't expect it to come cheap. And with the current generation of toolsets, don't expect it to work well, especially at first: all the tools will do *something* useful 'out of the box', but there's a steep learning-curve, and a lot of work to set up the right metamodels. You'll need to develop workarounds for the tools' inevitable flaws and limitations; and none of them cover the whole scope in an integrated way, so you'll also need to cover those gaps with manual processes and methodology. But despite all frustrations and fragilities, it's still better than trying to do architecture without toolset support.

Probably, anyway.

Application

- What documents, models and other artefacts do you create in your current architecture processes?
- What are the business purposes of each artefact?
- Who are the audiences and stakeholders for each artefact?
- What toolsets do you use to create, maintain and distribute each type of artefact?
- What 'toolset gaps' do you need to resolve in your architecture practice?

Resources

🏯 Overview of enterprise-architecture toolsets: see www.enterprise-architecture.info/EA_Tools.htm

🏯 Volere requirements: see www.volere.co.uk

📖 Volere requirements: Suzanne Robertson and James Robertson, *Managing the Requirements Process*, Addison-Wesley (1999)

PURPOSE – AN OVERVIEW

Summary

The purpose of architecture is to support the changing needs of the business. At the whole-of-enterprise level, a simple strategic plan will never be enough – it needs to cope with a much higher degree of dynamic complexity. And whilst IT-architecture often talks in terms of 'engineering the enterprise', a more useful metaphor here is that of the 'living enterprise' – purposive, pro-active and *self*-adapting to change.

Details

Architecture on purpose

One phrase we'll often hear in conjunction with enterprise architecture is 'business/IT alignment'. The idea is that somehow the architecture should bring the aims of each side of the divide into alignment with each other, into agreement with each other.

IT people being who they are, of course, there's a hidden tendency to assume that it's the business that should change, to align itself with the needs and aims of whatever systems the IT group wants to provide – or all too often, whatever the vendors want to sell... And business people being who *they* are, they're not likely to be happy about this – *at all*. Which is not surprising, because they're right: every activity begins and ends with a *business* purpose. In that sense, business always comes first – and *must* always come first.

More to the point, there can be no separation here, no 'us and them' – and especially no 'us *versus* them'. There's a natural tendency amongst IT folks to see themselves as 'special and different', but their role, in essence, is that of just one more support-function for the overall enterprise. The moment a sense of separation is introduced, the whole enterprise is put at risk.

> That supposed separation – and likewise the somewhat arrogant sense of 'special and different' – puts IT's place within the enterprise at risk, too. Many IT departments tend to view themselves as a sort of 'insourced supplier' to the enterprise, with separate IT strategies, separate IT-governance, and so on. But this is not a wise tactic for IT –

> kind of like sawing off the branch you're sitting on, in fact – because it invites the rest of the business to view IT as an *external* supplier, and hence a suitable target for *outsourcing*. In which case, bye-bye to many – most? – of the IT jobs; and hello to total confusion all round in a year or two, most likely...
>
> In short, if you want to be part of the enterprise, *be* part of the enterprise – don't present yourself as separate!

The other critical point here is around scope and scale. It's common for IT to describe its concerns in terms of planning, or at best in terms of strategy for example, one toolset-vendor recently re-badged its enterprise-architecture offering as 'IT strategic planning'. But this too can be a mistake. at the whole-of-enterprise level, because the scope is too large and too complex for anything as predictable as a plan. To see why this matters so much, it's worthwhile to take a brief detour through a matter of metaphor – because the way we choose to *view* the enterprise also delimits what we can do *in* the enterprise.

A matter of metaphor

The key distinction we need to note here is between two different metaphors:

- the enterprise as *machine*
- the enterprise as *living organism*

The first is the classic view of the enterprise: a kind of 'machine for making money', in the commercial context. It's the metaphor that underpins Zachman's assertion that the role of enterprise architecture is 'engineering the enterprise'; further back, it's the same metaphor beneath Frederick Taylor's century-old notion of 'scientific management' that gave birth to Henry Ford's autocracy of the assembly-line. Inspired by Ford's apparent success, state-Communist regimes applied the same metaphor to the social realm, with an almost religious faith in the desirability, efficacy and achievability of the 'five year plan'. We might note, though, that not one of those regimes has withstood the test of time ...

> And likewise, it seems, the 'five year plan' itself. A week or so ago, at a seminar run by one of the EA toolset-vendors, a speaker asked for a show of hands as to how many IT executives still had a five-year plan. Five years earlier, perhaps even three years, perhaps even two, pretty much everyone would have had a predefined plan. But this time not a single hand went up. Not *one*. Interesting...
>
> Much the same reason, I'd guess, as to why another colleague argues that the best strategy for IT is to *not have* a strategy – or no static strategy, at least.

> So what's changed? Nothing, really. It's just that people have at last
> begun to realise that the five-year plan doesn't work – more to the
> point, that it *can't* work in the real world. It never *has* worked – that's
> the bleak irony here...

There's no doubt that the machine-metaphor does sort-of work in simple contexts with minimal variance and minimal change – the kind of problems we used to deal with, for example, in the monolithic world of old-style mainframes in which Zachman's 'information systems architecture' first emerged. But that isn't the world we deal with now: what we need instead is a metaphor that *can* cope with complexity. Which is where the metaphor of the 'living enterprise' comes into the picture. Which in turn is the reason for a renewed emphasis on business-purpose.

There's a subtlety here that turns out to be extremely important: a machine may be built *for* a purpose, but it doesn't *have* a purpose of its own. Any purpose the machine may have must come from *outside* of itself: it has no intrinsic purpose *in* itself. Hence armies of external apparatchiks – otherwise known as 'consultants', in the business world – to do the thinking for the machine, and to provide its purpose. Yet the Taylorist trap is that this comforting illusion of 'control' comes at a cost, because response to change slows to a crawl. Which is not a survival tactic in a rapidly-changing world...

Contrast this with the metaphor of the 'living enterprise'. The idea has been around for quite a few years now, but has gained business momentum – in Britain at least – through the activities of Charles Handy and others on the RSA's 'Tomorrow's Company' group. (The Royal Society of Arts, Manufactures and Commerce – to give its full title – is the world's oldest formal business organisation, founded way back in the seventeenth century.) And it's arguable that the living-enterprise metaphor is the only one that works well at the whole-of-enterprise level.

The key concept is that the enterprise is viewed not as a collection of discrete, separate parts, but as a web of interdependent services, all sharing a common aim. None of the parts is inherently 'better' or more important than any other: each has their own role to play – so management provides 'management services' to the whole, HR provides 'people services', operations provide 'production services', and so on. In the living organisation, 'the brain of the firm' – to use the term coined by cyberneticist Stafford Beer – is not something separate, but is distributed throughout every aspect of the enterprise.

In this context, 'service-oriented architecture' is no longer just an IT-industry buzzword, but an accurate description of the entire enterprise. Stafford Beer's Viable System Model has been proven in practice for half a century as a successful framework to structure the information-flows – the metaphoric 'nerve-system' - of large, complex enterprises, up to the scale of an entire country in one case. 'Viable system' design principles, such as recursion and reflexion, can also be used for other whole-of-enterprise services such as infrastructure, energy-supply, quality-management, strategy, security, business-ethics and the like – the living-enterprise equivalents of skeleton, veins, arteries, endocrine system and so on – though we'll explore that in more depth in a later book in this series.

The whole is not just the sum of its parts – as it is in the machine-metaphor – but is *more* than the sum of its parts: and every part *matters*. We also see the same principles at work in other business-themes such as Six Sigma and Total Quality Management. When 'the machine' becomes *self*-directing, 'self-actualised', responses can become fast enough to cope with the real-time complexities and confusions of the real world. And the sense of purpose – an *internalised* sense of purpose – is what drives those responses, ensuring that each can be appropriate to context and need.

That clear sense of purpose also provides resilience, it seems. LloydsTSB Bank was an early adopter of the 'living enterprise' metaphor – and partly because of that, was one of the few large British banks to survive the 2008 'credit crunch' almost unscathed. Might be a useful lesson there for others in the finance industry, and elsewhere too, perhaps…

In the machine-metaphor, we try to take control of the enterprise, through predefined plans and strategies. But it doesn't work: all manner of proven reasons as to *why* it can't work, but the fact is that it doesn't. By contrast, in the living-enterprise metaphor, we don't even *try* to plan: instead, we provide *direction*, through purpose. In the same way, so-called 'city-planning' isn't about *planning* as such, but about direction, about purpose. At every scale, in every decision, every service, the purpose *defines* the enterprise – and that in itself is what makes all the difference.

Coping with complexity

As enterprise architects, charged with tackling so large a scope, how on earth *do* we cope with all that complexity? It's actually a lot simpler than it looks, as long as we remember two key points:

- don't try to do it all in one go
- work *with* the complexity, not against it

Although some of the lesser-known IT-architecture frameworks such as Sogeti's *DyA*, or 'Dynamic Architecture', do provide some help in this, most of the common frameworks fail on both counts – another reason why they can become recipes for expensive insanity at the *enterprise* level. John Zachman, for example, insists that everything about the entire enterprise should be recorded in "excruciating detail" – a worthy goal, perhaps, but not a realistic one, not least because it takes so long that the detail is out of date before we're even a tenth of the way through.

In a sense, though, Zachman is right. We *do* eventually need that level of detail – but *only* where we need it, not absolutely everywhere. We'll come back to this again when we look at methodology, but for now it's useful to compare two different approaches to understanding any large system: *analysis*, and *holism*.

Analytic assessment and holistic assessment

Conventional *analysis* breaks a large system into manageable chunks – 'eating the elephant one bite at a time' – by splitting each chunk into parts, and those into smaller parts, and so on. The emphasis is on identifying the detail of each item and its individual components. But the catch is that once we get down into the kind of low-level detail we need to solve real-world problems, it's all too easy to lose track of where each part fits within the whole. It's like if we cut up a photograph into small pieces: we're left with a jigsaw-puzzle of very fine detail, but no 'big-picture' to tie it all together. And because there's nothing to tie all the pieces together, analysis *demands* stability: if the world moves on whilst we're working on it, we're lost.

By contrast, an *holistic* approach is more like cutting up a holograph. Each tiny piece of the picture may seem blurry and indistinct, yet each maintains within itself a pattern of the whole. We still do assessments that *look* like analysis – often all the way down to Zachman's 'excruciating detail' – but the real emphasis is on *patterns*, and on connections *between* items rather than the items themselves. Each dive down in to the detail also provides a bit more certainty about the nature of the whole. And because everything is linked together from the start, we don't need certainty or stability: we *can* work on a changing world.

To make it work, we *start* with a 'big-picture' view. To put it bluntly, we make it up: it's an invention, nothing more than that. But we create it from what we can see of those aspects of the enterprise that don't change over time – particularly its guiding principles and values. These form the skeleton or backbone of the

25

framework for our 'holograph', to which we add more and more detail as we go.

How does this help us tackle what would otherwise be an overwhelming complexity? One answer is that we don't set out to create and impose some kind of top-down 'city master-plan': instead, we build the hologram iteratively, from every possible perspective, engaging the views and opinions of people at every level and in every domain. We may well need some kind of unifying design to start with – see 'The architecture cycle' in *Methodology – an overview*, p.108 – but as the architecture matures, we're probably better to adopt a more 'hands-off' approach – see *Methodology – hands-off architecture*, p.161.

The other answer, perhaps, is to use models that explicitly address the complexity – rather than shy away from it, as in the usual 'control'-based approach to enterprise architecture. For this, one of the most valuable models in our toolkit is one originally developed at IBM by Dave Snowden and others, called Cynefin.

Cynefin and complexity

Like all good models, Cynefin is deceptively simple. Given a context that seems unknown, it says, we have four ways to work with it: assume it's known; analyse it into something knowable; find some way to work *with* the emergent complexity; or accept the implicit uncertainty of a unique 'market of one'.

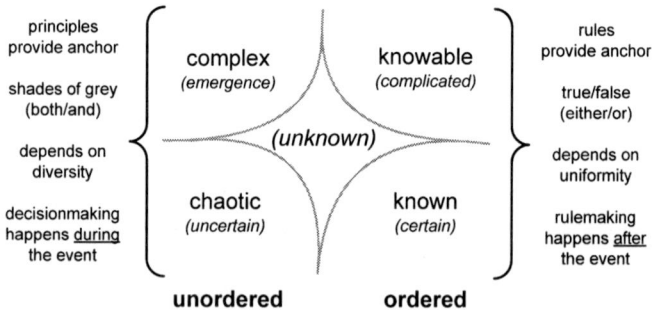

Cynefin model

Each domain has a different decision-making style:
- 'known' domain: based on predefined *rules*
- 'knowable' domain: based on *analysis*
- 'complex' domain: based on *guidelines* and heuristics
- 'chaotic' domain: based on *principles*

In a sense, these form a hierarchy. At the simplest rule-based level, we need know little or nothing about business-purpose: we just follow the rules. But as the world we deal with becomes more complex and chaotic, purpose matters more and more. Hence, again, why clarity on and alignment with business-purpose becomes ever more important as we expand the scope and complexity of the enterprise architecture.

Decision-making is fast in the 'known' and 'chaotic' domains, but require radically different levels of skill to be reliable; decision-making is slower in the 'knowable' and 'complex' domains, but at least we have a better idea of how we get there! More on this later when we look at mapping capabilities and decisions within the architecture-framework – see *Framework – primitives*, p.63.

Difficulties with dynamics

At the highest level of business-purpose, the Vision – as it's called in ISO-9000:2000 – identifies the core values and principles that define the enterprise. These never change – or perhaps more to the point, they're so much the core of the enterprise that if they *do* change, it's no longer the same enterprise.

> One of the classic examples of this is the 'HP Way', the original guiding principles for Hewlett-Packard. When those principles were in effect abandoned by a new management, quite soon after the founders' deaths, the company went into a steep decline, from which it seems still yet to recover.

But those core values are the only things that don't change in the enterprise, and in the enterprise architecture. Everything else *does* change. So we perhaps again need to hammer this point home:

The world is not static; there is no 'future state'

Talking about 'as-is' versus 'to-be' is fine, as far as it goes; but trying to define a 'future state' isn't, because there is no possible 'steady state' – especially not at the scope of whole-of-enterprise architecture.

One other trap here is the tendency to regard the organisation as '*the* enterprise'. It isn't. It's true that the organisation is an enterprise in its own right, but the *real* enterprise – the one we need to identify and model in our enterprise architecture – is a much more fluid, dynamic entity: more like 'enterprises' plural, in fact. Remember that definition earlier: an enterprise can be *any* kind of grouping, of *any* size or boundaries, sharing a common purpose within a common scope. It can be as small as a single work-team; it can be as large as an industry-wide consortium; ultimately, in certain contexts, it might well include the entire world. It's only at the very top that the purpose is static; over time, everything else will change its scope and boundaries and details of purpose, merging, demerging, in every possible combination. *Everything.* That's a lot of flexibility, a *lot* of change, all the time – but that's what real enterprise architecture demands.

Yes, it's complex – enormously so – and often with nightmare problems with versioning and the like. But it *is* doable, as long as we remember those two points: don't try to do it all in one go – because we can't – and do use that holistic overview to manage the dynamics of complexity.

Application

- How do you ensure an emphasis on business-purpose in your architecture?
- Who defines business-purpose for your architecture?
- How do you ensure business engagement in architecture development and use?
- How do you manage complexity and dynamics in your architecture?
- How do you ensure a balance between analysis and holistics in your architecture?

Resources

- FEAF: *A Practical Guide to Federal Enterprise Architecture*: see www.gao.gov/special.pubs/eaguide.pdf [PDF]
- TOGAF (The Open Group Architecture Framework): see www.opengroup.org/togaf
- RSA 'Tomorrow's Company' group: www.tomorrowscompany.com
- Viable System Model: see Wikipedia summary on en.wikipedia.org/wiki/Viable_System_Model
- DyA (Dynamic Architecture): see eng.dya.info/Home/
- Cynefin: Wikipedia overview at en.wikipedia.org/wiki/Cynefin; more detail at Cognitive Edge: www.cognitive-edge.com
- The 'HP Way' principles: see www.hpalumni.org/hp_way.htm

PURPOSE – BUSINESS-DRIVEN ARCHITECTURE

Summary

All architecture begins with a business-purpose, a business question to be addressed. These 'business drivers' can take many different forms, from 'top-down' strategy or 'bottom-up' impacts of real-world incidents, to routine replacements and re-engineering, or resolution of complex 'pain-points' for the business.

Details

If architecture-development is to be done 'on purpose', we first need to identify the applicable business-purpose – the 'business question' which the revised architecture should seek to resolve.

In effect, this business-question becomes both anchor-point and starting-point for the respective iteration of the architecture cycle (see 'The architecture cycle' in *Methodology – an overview*, p.108). It's useful, too, to categorise these drivers in terms of their location and thrust within the layers of the architecture framework (see *Framework – layers*, p.59): 'horizontal', 'top-down', 'bottom-up', and 'spiral-out'. In a sense, these categories also represent levels of architecture maturity, with horizontal drivers addressed early on, whilst the capability to handle the complexities of spiral-out drivers is usually available only at a higher level of maturity.

Horizontal drivers

'Horizontal' drivers such as optimisation and improved lifecycle management, especially for IT-systems and services, are the most common starting-points for architecture-development. These concerns initially touch the enterprise in the middle layers of the framework – typically at the 'logical' implementation-independent view of the enterprise – and usually spread horizontally across the framework (for example, assessing the impact of a rationalised data-structure on business-processes) before filtering downward in a controlled manner towards the operations space. Often there will be no apparent impact or need for architectural assessment at higher levels, other than for cost-management, or as reflected in improved performance. Examples include:

- rationalisation or optimisation of existing systems and services
- improved lifecycle-management
- standardisation of information-structures and information-sharing (data-warehouse, data-mart, etc)
- cost-reduction in a specific area and to a specific target

The architectural focus with horizontal concerns is to select a start-point for optimisation – such as rationalisation of data-structures, or simplification of some part of the IT-systems portfolio – and identify the implications of the resultant redesign on a selected scope within the enterprise, working downward on that broader front towards the operations space. As with top-down drivers, the requirements going outward and downward meet with the limits imposed by real-world constraints.

In early-maturity enterprise-architecture, the architects' task is usually to rationalise in one narrow-focus area, creating change-requirements within that space, and at best summarise the probable effects elsewhere. The danger, especially with conventional IT-centric 'enterprise'-architecture, is that the scope may not be broad enough to assess the full impact of the changes, resulting in a false 'optimisation' which reduces the optimisation of the whole. It's often left to solution-designers to identify and resolve the broader impacts of implementing the required changes into the operations space. In later-maturity architecture, the architects should build a more detailed map of effects and implications, as for top-down drivers.

Top-down drivers

'Top-down' drivers are concerns which initially touch the enterprise at a high level and expand their impact downwards towards the operations space, often eventually influencing a broad area of the enterprise. Examples include:

- change of strategy
- legislative or regulatory change
- market change
- business-transformation imperative such as overall cost-reduction or reduced-time-to-market
- unifying 'theme' such as quality, security, privacy, environment

The architectural focus with top-down concerns is to identify the driver's implications as they expand outward and downward at each successive layer. In effect, the desired or required change going downward meets with the limits imposed by real-world constraints moving up.

The architects' task is usually to build a map or audit-trail of connections and effects, and derive appropriate change-requirements at each layer. The solution-designers' task is to provide the maximum possible compliance to the requirements yet with the minimum practicable disruption.

Bottom-up drivers

'Bottom-up' drivers are potential or actual real-world incidents which initially touch the enterprise in the operations space and expand their effect upwards and outwards, impacting to a greater or lesser degree on performance, and sometimes in areas apparently far removed from the nominal incident. Examples include:

- replacement of hardware, software, equipment, etc
- operational issues such as machine downtime
- disaster-recovery planning
- risk management
- real-time incident-impact assessment and resolution

The architectural focus with bottom-up concerns is to identify the implications of the driver as they expand upward, outward and downward again at each successive layer. In effect, the real-world constraint ripples upward to impact on the imagined or desired 'as-is' or 'to-be' context for the enterprise. Unlike top-down drivers, which are always to some extent planned and future-focussed, bottom-up impacts may well be unexpected – though preferably designed-for – and may be triggered by real-time alerts.

The architects' task is usually to build a map or audit-trail of connections and probable impacts, and derive appropriate change-requirements at each layer. In risk-management or disaster-recovery planning, this will usually start with failure scenarios or simulations. The solution-designers' task is usually to provide fall-back capabilities that can deliver the required services under the specified failure-conditions with the minimum impact on overall performance. Architects and solutions-designers will need to work together to resolve the trade-offs between potential risks and the real-world constraints on holding capabilities in reserve.

Development of dialogue – see *Completion – closing the loop*, p.184 – is critical here, because there's no way we can plan for every eventuality in the real world. As with other pervasive concerns such as security or health and safety, what's most needed is an enhanced awareness of the issues amongst the people at the front-line – those who deal with the real world on a day-to-day, minute-by-minute basis. Prepackaged systems and disaster-recovery procedures are useful, of course, but in practice are often less important than people's ability to think out and apply an appropriate solution on-the-fly whilst still being aware of impact on the overall architecture.

Spiral-out drivers

'Spiral-out' drivers start at one particular point in the framework, such as an apparent problem in business reporting. They then spiral or 'pinball' outward in any direction from there, in some cases touching every cell in the framework. Examples include:

- identification and resolution of business 'pain-points' and other intractable problem-issues
- assessment of impact of planned implementation of innovations, such as enhanced technology or operational restructure
- complex interactions such as 'single source of truth'

The architectural focus with simpler spiral-out concerns such as technology enhancement is similar to horizontal concerns, but the scope is wider, and hence more reliable for the overall enterprise. For more complex spiral-out concerns such as 'pain-point' resolution, the initial focus is to identify the true source of the 'problem'-condition – which is rarely where it at first appears to be! (Often this is *why* the problem seems to be intractable, too.)

In both cases, architectural assessment will only succeed if the team has the authority to review *any* related aspect of the business – which will usually apply only in a more mature enterprise architecture associated with an enterprise-wide PMO rather than under the aegis of the IT domain alone. In effect, the 'problem-issue' is a real-world constraint that impacts on the imagined or desired 'as-is' or 'to-be' for the enterprise, similar to a 'bottom-up' driver, but its effect is usually first noticed at some point above the operations space.

> 'Pain' in a business sense can take many forms: sometimes avoidance of embarrassment at high levels can become a most immediate business driver.

> In one case we dealt with, government and opposition had all but come to blows over two different sets of figures for a government department, painting very different pictures of performance, but which supposedly came from the exact same source. Accusations of incompetence and worse flew around in the press: *not* happy…
>
> After a few angry phone calls from minister to department heads, and so on down the hierarchy, it turned out that everyone was right – sort of. Both sets of figures did come from the same source – sort of – but had gone through different transforms and business-rules, without any controlled audit-trail, ending up in different reporting-systems but purporting to be the same thing. Oops.
>
> We'd previously struggled to get the go-ahead for projects with abstract-sounding themes such as 'single source of truth' and 'database of record'. For a while, though, these seemed to gain a very high value – not far off a no-questions-asked business-case, in fact. Ours not to reason why…

The architects' task is usually an iterative process, analysing the issues at each point, then building a trail of connections, and analysing the impacts at the next point on the trail, following the trails of dependency and interaction as appropriate between cells and layers of the framework. Once the full map is constructed, the architects derive appropriate change-requirements for each layer. The solution-designers' task is often unusually complicated, especially for 'pain-point' concerns, because it's rare that the required changes would be confined to a single domain such as IT-systems. Solutions will often need a large proportion of human-based processes, even for nominal 'IT' issues. A broad 'business transformation' team, including architects, solutions-designers and many other specialists, will often be needed to work together to resolve the complex trade-offs and delicate political issues arising from these business-drivers.

As with the bottom-up drivers, creating a dialogue between all stakeholders is probably the most important aim here. An IT-centric architecture alone will rarely help: in fact poorly-thought-through IT-centric 'solutions' are some of the most common *causes* of intractable pain-points. Pain-points also often arise from mis-matched decision-making processes, creating 'meaning gaps' in which information is passed cleanly between processes but the *meaning* of that information may be lost. For IT-based systems especially, it's worthwhile checking decision-processes against the Cynefin categories – rule-based, analytic, heuristic, and principle-based – because IT can only handle the first category easily, the second expensively, the third rarely, and the fourth not at all: if a person is expected to fill the decision-gap, we need to make sure that they have the information and skills and ability to do so, otherwise it'll only make the problem worse! Understanding such meaning-gaps and value-gaps is critical for accurate gap-analysis – see 'Phase D – derive change-requirements' in *Methodology – assessment*, p. 140.

Application

- What are the business drivers in your enterprise?
- What are the business drivers for your architecture?
- How do you ensure those business drivers are tracked within your architecture?
- Who has ultimate responsibility for each business driver and its resolution?

Resources

Business drivers in TOGAF: see www.opengroup.org/architecture/togaf8-doc/arch/toc.html (chapters 'Phase B: Business Architecture' and 'Business Scenarios')

Requirements in TOGAF: see www.opengroup.org/architecture/togaf8-doc/arch/toc.html (chapter 'ADM Architecture Requirements Management')

David Robertson et al., *Enterprise Architecture as Strategy: creating a foundation for business execution* (Harvard Business School Press, 2006)

GOVERNANCE – AN OVERVIEW

Summary

Governance addresses the people-issues around the 'who' and 'why' of enterprise-architecture: who does what, who is responsible for what, and why things should be and have been done. The system for governance provides formal structure for the processes that manage these issues.

Details

Architecture and the enterprise

In terms of creating a governance structure that works for enterprise architecture, one of the hardest problems – that of establishing where architecture sits within the enterprise – arises because of architecture's history. Back in the bad old days, a decade or so ago, architecture was regarded solely as a means to resolve some of the nightmarish messes in low-level technology – particularly the tangle of proprietary systems and incompatible interfaces. As those issues were brought under control, the concerns moved upward, to IT-architecture at an enterprise wide scale; and eventually to a belated awareness that business-needs must be included in the architecture equation. But throughout, there was always an implicit assumption of 'enterprise architecture' as part of IT, and that it belongs under the aegis of IT governance.

The catch is that it *isn't* a subset of IT – it's part of the *enterprise*, of which IT is merely one component. Hence, no matter what IT and the CIO or CTO may think, it *doesn't* belong under their authority. This can cause huge problems around governance, because once we reach a true enterprise-wide scope, we may find ourselves in a situation in which governance-mechanisms for a small subset of the enterprise are forced to try to take control of the whole enterprise.

> One common outcome of IT-centric governance is that broad-scope issues are tackled from far too narrow a perspective. For example, in an interview in early 2008 in the *British Medical Journal*, a key player in the National Health Service IT programme described the resultant 'detachment' between the programme leads and health professionals:

"It was originally seen as [an IT-specific] contracting process. That's why they brought in an ace contractor to run it. Then it was seen as a technology project".

Three years and many, many millions of pounds later, someone at last recognised that other stakeholders than IT really did need to be involved: "they realised they needed to get clinical engagement". But even then the effort to bring the end-users on board was not only "late and under-resourced", but crippled by unrealistic technology-centric assumptions: as one of the clinical leads put it, "we had to persuade [IT] that throwing out the entire base accumulated over twenty years was not a good idea"...

When the scope needs to be enterprise-wide, so must the governance. At some point, architecture needs to move out of IT and upward, often as a support for an enterprise-wide programme-management office, or equivalent, which ideally would report direct to the CEO, not the CIO or CTO. And if IT won't relinquish control at this point, relations between business and IT will rapidly worsen: business stakeholders accuse IT of trying to 'take over' the whole enterprise, whilst IT-architects complain about increased workloads and increasingly 'uncooperative' business clients. It's not a happy sight.

There's an even less happy outcome that I've seen several times. It can occur if architects feel so threatened by the change that they withdraw further and further back into the 'safe' IT-centric space, retreating into an obsession with architectural 'purity' that takes precedence over any real-world needs. The result, often painfully prolonged over months or years, is that the architecture-team fades into irrelevance; and they're bypassed so often, out of sheer business necessity, that even the operational architecture eventually falls apart – with serious consequences for the enterprise. So let's emphasise this point again:

If any aspect of architecture has enterprise-wide scope, it must have enterprise-level governance.

A corollary to this is that if the architecture has enterprise-wide implications, it needs to be backed by enterprise-level authority. For redesigns of end-to-end processes to work, for example, architects *must* be able to bridge across every aspect of the enterprise – yet many of the silo-walls around individual fiefdoms may be so strongly defended that it'd take the imprimatur of the entire executive to breach them.

In short, the backing of the CIO alone – or further down the abstraction scale, that of the CTO – is never going to be enough for the kind of work we're describing here. For whole-of-enterprise architecture, if you don't have the full and active support of at least the CEO behind you, it's best to forget the whole thing and go home. As simple as that. Which means that you'll first need to convince the CEO that EA *is* valuable and useful...

Governance drivers

The purpose of enterprise-architecture governance is to address its 'who' and 'why': who does what, who is responsible for what, and why things should be done, are done, and have been done.

From an internal perspective, the drivers for governance include:

- *universals*: the overlighting vision, values and principles of the enterprise as a whole – which, as with architecture, always exist in some form, even if they're implicit or dysfunctional...
- *policy*: the choices and guidelines arising from those 'universals', particularly in how they impact on people's choices, actions and incentives or disincentives
- *strategy*: the choices and guidelines that drive and underpin operational and cultural change, and how appropriate changes are chosen, promoted, promulgated and managed

Other, more 'external' drivers for governance include:

- *compliance* with legislation, regulation and shared standards: either imposed from 'outside', by governments or trade regulators, or in response to pressure-groups and others – perhaps voluntarily, such as with standards or interface specifications shared across a consortium or an entire industry
- *accountability*: should support a shared sense of responsibility rather than any kind of 'blame game', and ideally also aligned with better management of shared knowledge and experience
- *transparency*: strongly linked to accountability, though often also aligned to the enterprise's need for reputation-management with shareholders and other stakeholders

Whatever structure of governance we put in place for our enterprise architecture, it needs to address all of those drivers above. Not easy – but necessary nonetheless.

Governance styles and standards

Perhaps the most common view of governance is that it provides management with a sense of *control* over what's happening, in the architecture or whatever. This assumption is reflected in the names of governance- and project-management frameworks, such as PRINCE2 (PRojects IN *Controlled* Environments) and COBIT (*Control* OBjectives in Information and related Technology).

But unfortunately, as the Cynefin model makes clear, in the real world there is no such thing as 'control'. It's a myth, a dangerous delusion – especially in the contexts we deal with in enterprise architecture, so often typified by rapid change, and in which the only certainty is that the situation will always be somewhat uncertain. So we need a form of governance for architecture that, to quote the TOGAF specification, is "less about overt control and strict adherence to rules, and more about guidance and effective and equitable usage of resources to ensure sustainability of an organisation's strategic objectives". Which isn't easy, because so many people seem to *need* that delusion of 'control'...

The hard part is to find the right balance between discipline and flexibility, between centralisation in a specialist elite versus a more open involvement of all potential stakeholders. The classic 'water-fall' approach provides formal structure, but often with excessive rigidity, whilst some supposed Agile models end up little better than an excuse for an undisciplined free-for-all – the exact anti-thesis of architecture. The complexities of 'need to know, need to use' should not be underestimated, either: inadequate sharing of models and other architectural information will cause problems, but a system that is open to everyone often turns out to be a security nightmare.

The approach I've used here, based in part on PRINCE2 and TOGAF (see *Methodology and governance*, p.106), does give a reasonable trade-off between the various competing factors, and should serve at least as a starting-point for governance design.

> Note that this is for governance of *architecture* only. Governance of projects and change-programmes, and for that matter of IT and other technology issues, is outside its scope, although it does need to intersect with that broader governance at various phases of the architecture cycle.

In this model, the governance is embedded into the architecture methodology, with stakeholder reviews and other PRINCE2 style 'products' (see *Governance – products*, p.48) providing guidance and marking the boundaries of the cycle's phases. Ideally, the stakeholders for each entity and other aspects of the architecture should be identified automatically by the toolset, via links in the architecture-repository; it takes a fair amount of effort to set up and maintain, but is well worth doing, if only because it so much simplifies the security and access-control concerns.

But the fine detail of governance will always depend in part on your enterprise's context: you'll always need to 'roll your own' to some extent. The best approach is always to look closely at your own context's needs, then start off with what standards and governance you have, and build outward from there.

Governance in the multi-partner enterprise

Governance for architecture is hard enough when the enterprise fits within one domain of one organisation, as is usually the case for IT-architecture. As above, the complexities increase when governance needs to cover a wider scope than that single domain of IT; but they increase many times over as soon as the enterprise moves beyond the bounds of a single organisation.

The reason for the increased complexity comes down to one word: jurisdiction. Governance – or at least the *semblance* of governance – will seem relatively easy if we can issue edicts from on high and can expect them to be followed with little question, as we might do within a single organisation. Not so in the multi-partner enterprise: formal contracts and other forms of 'enforcement' are important, of course, but will often slow things down to the point where they become unworkable. Instead, everything has to be negotiated, maintained by trust, by careful communication, by relationships and responsibilities (see *Governance – roles and responsibilities*, p.41). In short, don't even try to create a broad-scope architecture unless you're willing to deal with delicate diplomacy across the whole range of stakeholders.

Some of the issues you'll need to address include:

- *stakeholders and style*: who are the stakeholders? how will you communicate with each stakeholder or group of stakeholders? will you use an 'open' or 'closed' model, a waterfall-style or agile-style?
- *security and knowledge-sharing*: how will you manage access-control and other issues of 'need to know, need to use'? how will you ensure that each stakeholder does have access to the information they need, when they need it? how do you ensure that the voice of every stakeholder can be heard, without slowing everything down to where you risk losing the gains of broader engagement?
- *scheduling, change-management and other dynamics*: how will you track and manage cross-dependencies between systems and processes? how will you manage different rates of change between the partners in the enterprise?

None of this is all that different to what needs to apply in any multi-partner consortium for a large shared project. What *is* different is that it's not a 'project' – it's a *process*, an ongoing capability. And what makes it *really* complicated is that the boundaries of 'the enterprise' are themselves changing all the time – different partners, stakeholders, technologies, markets, needs and concerns. Only by starting from the awareness that it *is* so, and designing our governance accordingly from the start, do we have any chance of coping with those levels of complexity.

Application

- Where does enterprise-architecture sit within your enterprise?
- Who manages governance of enterprise-architecture?
- What governance models, frameworks, tools and methodologies do you use for enterprise-architecture in your enterprise?
- What governance is used for change-management in your enterprise?

Resources

- Cynefin and complexity: see [href: link]www.cognitive-edge.com and Wikipedia summary at en.wikipedia.org/wiki/Cynefin
- COBIT: see www.isaca.org/cobit/
- PRINCE2 (PRojects In Controlled Environments): see www.ogc.gov.uk/methods_prince_2.asp
- Governance in TOGAF: see www.opengroup.org/architecture/togaf8-doc/arch/toc.html (chapter 'Architecture Governance')
- Governance of Agile methodologies: see agilemanifesto.org and www.agilealliance.org

GOVERNANCE – ROLES AND RESPONSIBILITIES

Summary

The 'who' issues of architecture-governance revolve around roles and responsibilities: who is responsible for what, in what sequence, and why. Keeping the business-purpose in mind at all times is essential here – as is an awareness that people need to be respected *as* people, and not as machines subject to governance 'control'.

Details

Roles and responsibilities – an overview

Governance is about the 'who' and 'why' of architecture – which means we need to be able to identify and track who does what, who is responsible for what, and ensure that each know what is expected of them in order to make the architecture work for the whole of the enterprise.

Most of this is similar to what would be familiar in IT architecture: the key themes are described well in the respective parts of the TOGAF specification, under its sections such as 'Architecture Governance Framework' and 'Architecture Charter'. The main extensions we need to deal with here are to do with the *people*-aspects of the issues. We can assign responsibility to someone via their role, for example, but that's not going to mean anything if they don't *know* what they need to do in support of the architecture – or for that matter if they don't even know they *have* that role, which I've seen happen in all too many circumstances.

> Another key concern here is handover of responsibilities whenever someone leaves or joins the enterprise, or simply changes role. It's not a trivial issue: at a true enterprise-wide scale for architecture, there may well be several significant stakeholders changing roles every day.
>
> A few organisations I've worked with have integrated these aspects of knowledge-management fully into their architecture-governance processes; but most don't seem to do even a straightforward exit-interview, or in some cases be aware of the need for such things at all.

> So what processes and systems exist in your enterprise to support this
> kind of knowledge-transfer? – because if you *don't* have an appropriate
> system in place to capture and transfer this knowledge from person to
> person, your architecture will be in danger from Day One.

Remember that in a multi-partner enterprise, or any part of the
enterprise which is outside of your direct jurisdiction, relationships with your stakeholders will be via negotiation and communication rather than any simple form of enforcement. So to
make it work with your stakeholders, you're going to have to
provide conditions under which they *want* the architecture to
succeed. It's up to you to make it important to them – which isn't
always easy, especially in the earlier stages of promoting a
broader enterprise-wide architecture.

What *doesn't* work is heavy-handed 'policing'. Instead, aim for at
least some of the following:

- *cross-project synergies*: review and cross-reference project
  architecture documents (see, for example, *Architecture
  Compliance Statement*, p.175) to identify ways in which projects
  can support each other – providing savings in complexity,
  time and budget
- *inter-project negotiation*: offer to assist in identifying trade-offs
  from a 'big-picture' perspective, where projects have
  conflicting needs and constraints
- *personal contact*: keep in direct contact with all key
  stakeholders, especially project-managers and project-leads, to
  pre-empt any risks of miscommunication or isolation

Note that many of your stakeholders from the business or
operations space may be wary of a broader enterprise-wide architecture, especially if the enterprise suffers from an apparent
'IT/business divide'. It's worthwhile reminding yourself that, as
an IT-architect, many of your architecture stakeholders will be
dealing with constraints and trade-offs of which you may have
had little or no practical experience: a little humility from you will
often go a long way in gaining their trust and respect!

Identifying the stakeholders

Like the architecture itself, identifying the relevant stakeholders is
likely to be an iterative process. The key concept here is that of
ownership – not in the usual sense of possession of something, but
more in terms of a declared and acknowledged responsibility.

Assets, records, processes, events, documents, business-rules and
all manner of other business-items each have an *owner* – the

'responsible person'. Other groups of stakeholders create, read and otherwise use the respective items. And although there are specific points within the methodology where we search for such stakeholders and their changing roles (see *Methodology – assessment*, p.121), keeping track of all these people is *hard* – especially in a multi-partner enterprise.

For a number of reasons, the best place to keep this information is in the architecture repository – not least because that's where we'll be looking anyway when we want to identify the business scope for an architecture cycle (see *Phase A – establish iteration scope*, p.122). So it's almost essential that the toolset we use (see *Basics – artefacts and toolsets*, p.17) can support links to this kind of metadata – either 'out of the box', or by modifying the underlying metamodel. That way, each time we scan through the framework in the architecture repository, we automatically gather together a list of probable stakeholders for the respective scope.

The main complication is that despite the key notion of having only a single 'responsible person' for each item, in most cases we end up with multiple stakeholders and even multiple 'owners' for any given context. This occurs because we need to ensure that there are owners for each of the key 'primitives' such as an asset or a data-item or a business-rule (see *Primitives versus composites*, p.55); but there also need to be distinct owners for each of the business-processes and other 'composites' in which those primitives are used, and for the higher-level products and services which use those composites, and so on, layer upon layer. In many contexts we may end up with dozens of owners, each with their own prerogatives, concerns and constraints. This is one reason why the simplistic composite-only frameworks in many of the common IT-architecture metamodels can be such a problem (let alone the equally common and even more simplistic misuse of the basic primitive-only Zachman framework) – they provide no means to cope with this complex layering or relationships and responsibilities.

We also need to distinguish between the ultimate 'responsible person' at each layer – whose input we'll definitely need for any change of architecture – and those who assist in creating or changing the item, or use the item, or merely need to know about any changes. Which is where two ugly acronyms – RACI and CRUD – come into the picture.

RACI, CRUD and other matters

The purpose of RACI and CRUD is to clarify the governance concern (and for that matter, security concern) of 'need to know, need to use'. During the assessment phases of the methodology we'll need to build RACI- and CRUD-matrices for each of the stakeholders or groups identified via the information we hold in the architecture-repository.

The RACI categories describe 'need to know':

- *responsible* (i.e. 'accountable') – the business-owner of the item (there should be exactly one person with this assignment for each item)
- *assists* – those who assist the responsible person in managing the item, and may do the bulk of the work
- *consulted* – those whose opinions may be sought concerning the item (two-way communication)
- *informed* – those who need to be kept up-to-date on changes concerning the item (one-way communication)

Some variants of RACI matrices also identify stakeholder-groups who would *not* need to be consulted or informed of changes – for example, senior managers usually do not need to know about low-level details of operational changes.

The CRUD categories deal with 'need to use':

- *create* – those who create new instances of the item-type
- *read* – those who read or otherwise use the item or item-type instance without actually changing it
- *update* – those who read the item or instance, but who may also change it or its contents
- *delete* – those whose role may manage the deletion or destruction of instances of the item-type (and even of the item-type itself, though this would be far less common), and are likely also to be involved in overall lifecycle management for the items

Again, there are several variants or additions to the CRUD categories – such as for managers who may not need to know about individual items yet who *are* concerned with counts and averages and other aggregates of the items. But the standard CRUD list will usually suffice for first-level definitions for governance.

Partitioning the responsibilities

With an appropriate mechanism to track responsibilities and roles, you then need a formal structure for architecture governance. You might use an ISO9000-style structure, or ITIL, or COBIT, or PRINCE2 and MSP: as usual, it all depends on the context.

In the absence of any already-existing governance framework, the TOGAF model is a good place to start. The TOGAF specification includes a fairly comprehensive summary of the different aspects of governance, including architecture boards, governance processes, and key documents such as the Architecture Charter and Architecture Principles. The only catch is that all their descriptions are IT-centric – for example, the absurd assertion that governance for enterprise-architecture is a subset of IT-governance – so you will need to do a certain amount of translation to make it usable for real-world enterprise-architecture. The simplest way to do this translation is to remember that what TOGAF calls 'enterprise architecture' is at best enterprise-wide *IT*-architecture – in other words domain-architecture, not *enterprise* architecture. If you move the governance descriptions up a couple of notches in scope beyond the TOGAF assumptions, it should all start to make sense.

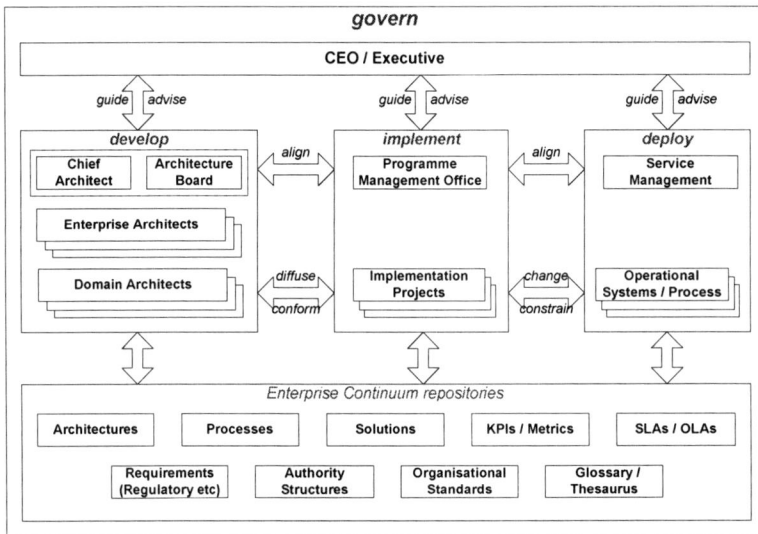

TOGAF-style structure of governance relationships

As the diagram indicates, we can more usefully separate architecture governance into four distinct segments, which each come to the fore in different aspects of the architecture process:

- *govern* – the highest level of governance within the enterprise
- *develop* – governance of the architecture itself
- *implement* – governance of implementing architected change in the enterprise
- *deploy* – governance of the use of architected changes

The **govern** segment has oversight of all other governance, including enterprise-architecture and the various domain-architectures. The high-level processes, standards and other guidance-documents for architecture are defined or reviewed in the Preparation phase of the methodology (see *Methodology – preparation*, p.113). At this level, the architecture-governance board should be headed by the CEO, or some other delegate with a whole-of-enterprise remit – *not* by the CIO or CTO (as per TOGAF), or for that matter the CFO or anyone else whose role is constrained to a single domain within the enterprise.

The **develop** segment has oversight of all of the development and management of the architecture. This particularly applies during the 'assessment' section of the architecture-cycle – Phases A to D in the methodology (see *Methodology – assessment*, p.121)

The **implement** segment has oversight of the processes of turning architectural overviews and ideas into practical solutions for the business needs identified in each architecture cycle. This segment is emphasised during the 'solution' section of the architecture-cycle – Phases E to H of the methodology (see *Methodology – solutions*, p.146). Although much if not most of this activity occurs in programme-management and change-management rather than architecture, the architecture should be referenced increasingly as the architecture-maturity is further developed.

The **deploy** segment has oversight of the operations space. This has little *direct* connection with the architecture-cycle as such, though links do occur in the 'lessons learned' reviews in Phase H, at the end of the cycle, and in the 'as-built' review in hands-off architecture (see *Methodology – hands-off architecture*, p.161), to garner feedback around what needs to change within the architecture (see *Completion – closing the loop*, p.184). However, many of the business-drivers for architecture-cycles may arise from this space, such as in risk-management and business-continuity planning, or resolution of 'pain-points' (see 'Bottom-up drivers' and 'Spiral-out drivers' in *Purpose – business-driven architecture*, p.29). With an appropriate toolset, and capabilities to monitor live activities in the operations space, the architecture may even be involved in real-time impact-analysis for incident-response.

The architecture repository – TOGAF's 'Enterprise Continuum' – is fundamental to all of this. It tracks all of the roles and responsibilities for governance; it presents a central reference-point for all the core documents and process-descriptions; and it provides a place in which to monitor and record all architecture-related governance activities, from within every aspect of the enterprise. It needs to be available to and shared by *everyone* for whom architecture is relevant in their work.

Application

- How do you identify architecture roles, responsibilities and stakeholders in your enterprise?
- What is the respective 'need to know, need to use' for each stakeholder, for each key item-type, and for architectural deployment of each item-type?
- How do you assign and verify architecture roles and responsibilities?
- How do you manage changes in those roles and responsibilities?

Resources

- Governance in ISO9000: see www.itgovernance.co.uk and Wikipedia summary at en.wikipedia.org/wiki/Iso_9000
- ITIL: see www.itil-officialsite.com
- COBIT: see www.isaca.org/cobit/
- MSP (Managing Successful Programmes): see www.ogc.gov.uk/guidance_managing_successful_projects.asp
- PRINCE2 (PRojects In Controlled Environments): see www.ogc.gov.uk/methods_prince_2.asp
- Governance in TOGAF: see www.opengroup.org/architecture/togaf8-doc/arch/toc.html (chapter 'Architecture Governance')

GOVERNANCE – PRODUCTS

Summary

Much of governance – in PRINCE2 especially – is monitored through 'products', the artefacts that record the outcomes of processes. This section summarises the various types of architecture products and their roles.

Details

Documents and other 'products' – an overview

Architecture is about structure, about *ideas,* and the processes of turning those ideas into concrete reality. One of the complications of enterprise-architecture is that, unlike physical architecture, so much of it exists only at the 'meta-level', as a kind of structure of structures, ideas about ideas, without any obvious tangible form. And without tangible form, it can be hard to manage.

Documents and other architecture 'products' fill this governance gap. Governance in the PRINCE2 project-management methodology, for example, is driven not through predefined processes, but by tracking roles and responsibilities and actions through documents produced within those processes – hence 'products'. We can categorise these products and related artefacts as follows:

- *guidance* products – for overall guidance of architecture
- *management* products – to track and monitor the architecture processes
- *reference* products – the tangible outcomes of architecture, used in other activities throughout the enterprise
- *metrics* products – reports, dashboards and other indicators to monitor architecture status and performance

The sheer range and volume and interdependencies of all these architecture products are key reasons why a proper purpose-built toolset is so essential for large-scale enterprise-architecture – see *Basics – artefacts and toolsets,* p.17. In addition to the summaries of the different categories of products here, you'll find more detail on product-content in the later section on architecture integration and completion – see *Completion – architecture artefacts,* p.169.

Guidance products

Several documents will need to exist to guide the overall process and purpose of architecture. These products include:

- *Architecture Charter* – authorises the architecture activity and defines the relevant roles and responsibilities in relation to the overall enterprise
- *Architecture Principles* – outlines policies and principles against which all architectural decisions may be assessed
- *Architecture Procedures* – outlines or specifies the processes and procedures to be followed in conducting architecture activities
- *Architecture Standards* – outlines or specifies the reference standards to be used for compliance in all architecture designs

In many cases these products will be layered, in the sense that an IT-architecture principles document, for example, should usually draw on and reference an overarching set of architecture principles defined within a higher organisation-wide document. This layering can be problematic in multi-partner enterprises because of the many ways in which differing jurisdictions may overlap or conflict – see 'Governance in the multi-partner enterprise' in *Governance – an overview*, p.39.

Management products

A significant number of products will need to be created and updated at various stages of the architecture-cycle, to govern the processes of the methodology and its outcomes. These include:

- *Request for Architecture Work* – the formal request that initiates an architecture-cycle
- *Statement of Architecture Work* – defines the context and 'project-plan' for a specific architecture-cycle
- Phase-completion reports – summarises or details the work done, for stakeholder review
- *Architecture Compliance Statement* – created by project-managers during preparation for implementation, to confirm that they have taken architectural imperatives into account in solution-designs
- Requirements – records of business-requirements, functional requirements, performance, user-interface and other qualitative requirements, and links between these and the related designs, implementations, tests and the like

- Issues, opportunities and risks – records of relevant concerns arising during the architecture-cycle, which may have impact either later in the cycle or have broader or longer-term scope

Some of these – particularly the cycle-plans and the phase completion reports – may be created and maintained as separate documents, but should ideally be held and derived from the architecture repository within the toolset. Other items such as requirements, issues and risks should *only* be held within a controlled repository, either within a separate purpose-built toolset, or preferably within the architecture toolset itself: in practice, anything less – such as separate spreadsheet files for each project or architecture cycle – is just too much risk, and prevents accurate tracking and cross-referencing.

As with the guidance documents, several of these products will be layered – project requirements derived from enterprise-wide standards, for example, or issues and risks arising from shared concerns about technology strategy.

Reference products

Most of the products of architecture and the architecture-cycles are used for reference in some form or other, such as:

- frameworks, metamodels and schemas to define item-types
- specifications and metadata to define item-instances
- models and item-lists linking item-instances and placing them within appropriate contexts
- analysis and cross-reference reports derived from items, models and related sources
- common glossary and thesaurus

From a governance perspective, all of these will need version-control and access-control on a 'need to know, need to use' basis. Every product will need a responsible 'owner', and there will need to be clear processes and procedures to manage creation, cross-referencing, amendment and deletion for every item and type of item. In most cases, these items should be stored and maintained within the shared architecture-repository of a purpose-built toolset: anything less will, again, place the value and integrity of the architecture at risk.

The cross-referencing between products may well become complex in the extreme, because of the inherently dynamic nature of the versions and cross-dependencies of each of the underlying items. This becomes even more complex in cases where, for security or confidentiality reasons, items need to be stored in separate but interlinked repositories, or have cross-dependencies with differing visibilities for different stakeholder-groups – circumstances which may well occur in multi-partner enterprises.

A related though usually less contentious issue of governance relates to choice of architecture frameworks, because they guide how items are interpreted – in other words, what items *mean*, in a business sense. These too are often layered, both in the key distinction between 'primitives' and 'composites' (see 'Primitives versus composites' in *Framework – an overview*, p.55), and also in relationships between what TOGAF describes as the 'architecture continuum' from 'foundation architectures' and shared industry-specific architectures to the individual architectures specific to a single enterprise or single portfolio within an enterprise. This can be particularly problematic in a multi-partner enterprise, because agreement on a shared set of descriptions of solution-components – composites – may be rendered meaningless without alignment of the metamodels for the low-level primitives underlying those composites. Care does need to be taken here, especially when migrating a former IT-centric 'enterprise architecture' to a true enterprise-wide scope.

Metrics products

In addition to the formal stage-reports from the methodology, there are a wide variety of status-indicators and other performance metrics that may be relevant to governance. These include:

- statistical reports
- intranet-based dashboards and other 'live' status-reports
- maturity-models

Some of these, such as the statistical reports, may be derived directly from the architecture-repository and other sources within the toolset. A few toolsets also support 'dashboards' that provide a visual summary of activity and the status of critical success-factors and performance-indicators, driven by data sourced from internal architecture-cycle records, or, in some cases even drawn bottom-up from linkages with automated activity-scanning systems in the operations space.

Proper governance of architecture will also require regular assessment against some kind of verified maturity-model. Although no such model seems as yet to cover the full whole-of-enterprise space, several models do exist for IT-architecture – such as the DyA Architecture Maturity Matrix and the matrix in the TOGAF specification – and are probably usable as an initial base once allowance is made for any inappropriate IT-centrism.

> I like Marlies van Steenbergen's *DyA Architecture Maturity Matrix*: it's solid, comprehensive and not too IT-centric. What it's not suitable for, however, is the initial stages of setting up an architecture capability: we achieved an embarrassing zero for both 'before' and 'after' scores after three months' hard work at a somewhat difficult client, because the model takes a fairly advanced capability as its assumed starting-point.
>
> Fortunately, a bit of searching on the web turned up the Meta Group's two-part *Architecture Maturity Audit* – which *is* suited to measuring the early stages of architecture development. That gave us 'before' and 'after' scores of 22.8% and 35.2% respectively – which validated our assertion that we had achieved *some* improvement over that period!

Once again, the IT-centrism of most existing 'enterprise architecture' frameworks, methodologies and toolsets can be a real hindrance to governance here, as it's hard to provide meaningful measures and statistics when the available metrics cover only a small subset of the overall scope. It's an issue that needs to be addressed with some urgency by toolset-vendors and other key players in the field if whole-of-enterprise architecture is to garner the support that it needs in the future.

Application

- What products and other artefacts are created and used within your current governance?
- How and by whom are each of these products used?
- Who has responsibility for each artefact?

Resources

- TOGAF architecture products: see www.opengroup.org/architecture/togaf8-doc/arch/toc.html (chapter 'ADM Input and Output Descriptions')
- TOGAF maturity model: see www.opengroup.org/architecture/togaf8-doc/arch/toc.html (chapter 'Architecture Maturity Models')
- DyA Architecture Maturity Matrix: see eng.dya.info/Home/services/architecture_maturity_model.zip
- Martin van den Berg and Marlies van Steenbergen, *Building an Enterprise Architecture Practice: tools, tips, best practices, ready-to-use insights* (Sogeti / Springer Verlag, 2006)
- Meta Group's Architecture Maturity Audit: *Meta Group Practice*, (2000), Vol 4 No.4 (for Part 1) and No.5 (for Part 2)

FRAMEWORK – AN OVERVIEW

Summary

The framework provides a means to categorise and cross-reference the various business-entities identified in the architecture. Because the framework also determines the business meaning of each entity, the well-known IT-centric frameworks such as Zachman and the FEAF Reference Architecture can be problematic for whole-of-enterprise architecture: at the root-level especially, the framework *must* always cover the whole scope of the enterprise, not just its IT.

Details

Taxonomy, ontology and other tortuous terms

The framework describes the 'what' of the architecture. And of all the frameworks for enterprise-architecture, Zachman's is perhaps *the* best-known artefact in the entire field. It consists of six horizontal rows or layers, representing different strategic or tactical perspectives (see *Framework – layers*, p.59); and six vertical columns, representing key categories of entities (see *Framework – primitives*, p.63). Between them they form thirty-six cells, each of which is supposed to represent a single type of indivisible 'primitive' which can be used to describe entities for compliance and re-use in the architecture.

	What	How	Where	Who	When	Why
Scope						
Business						
System						
Technology						
Implement						
Operations						

The Zachman framework

Looking at Zachman, it's easy to form the impression that it's a list of 'things' the business needs: data, processes, applications, locations, physical objects such as servers, routers and networks. Tick off the boxes, drop the items in the right pigeonholes, and that's your enterprise-architecture pretty much done, isn't it?

Uh... not quite... More like a *long* way from done, in fact, because the framework is much more than a set of boxes: it's what determines *meaning* in the architecture. The key issues here include two tangled terms: taxonomy, and ontology.

Taxonomy – literally 'the naming of arrangement' – identifies the ways in which items are organised and categorised within the architecture. It also specifies and determines the recognised or 'legal' relationships *between* items. Zachman's framework provides a useful overview-taxonomy for architectures, but in itself it's all but meaningless – literally so – because it provides no real ontology for that framework.

Ontology – literally 'the study of meaning' – expands on or links to a taxonomy by assigning agreed meanings to each of the items within it. There are a variety of forms this might take:

- *glossary* or 'controlled vocabulary' – a list of agreed terms applied to those items
- *thesaurus* – a list of agreed relationships between those terms
- *schema* – a list of item-types, the attributes and attribute-types associated with each item-type, and relationships and dependencies between item-types
- *metamodel* – a variant of a schema which usually includes visual representations of how the items and their relationships should be portrayed

Ideally, a glossary and thesaurus should be structured around a formal syntax, though it's not always essential (see 'Glossary and Thesaurus' in *Completion – architecture artefacts*, p.182). Schemas and metamodels should always follow a formal syntax, as they determine the structure of the architecture repositories and other stores (see 'Repositories' in *Completion – architecture artefacts*, p.179).

All of these items need to be maintained under explicit governance. In the architecture methodology, the main governance activity occurs in the Preliminary Phase prior to any architecture-cycle, or in regular formal reviews of the entire architecture (see *Methodology – preparation*, p.113). Context-specific reviews may also take place during the 'lessons learned' stage in the final phase of the architecture-cycle (see 'Phase H – review lessons-learned' in *Methodology – solutions*, p.157).

Primitives versus composites

In the architecture repository especially, metamodels tend to be stacked on top of each other in layers. In part this reflects the different views of the enterprise, as in Zachman's framework, and the different ways in which the various models and entities are used. But at the root, the key distinction here is between two different architectural functions, described by Zachman as *primitives* and *composites*.

The simplest analogy is that primitives are the atoms or root-elements of the architecture. Like molecules, the composites are architectural solution-components constructed from any required combination of simpler entities. Composites may often be layered, in the same way as a complex molecule such as DNA is itself structured from simpler molecules. As with DNA, re-structuring a composite, or changing some of its components, will change its function, perhaps to better suit a changed environment. Yet ultimately it needs to be possible to resolve every composite all the way down to its distinct elements, its root-primitives. This is crucial, because, as Zachman explains:

Primitive models are architecture.
Composite models are implementations.

Every composite is a pre-packaged 'solution' for something. Composites guide solution-architecture: for example, the 'Solutions Continuum' in the TOGAF reference framework is made up of layer upon layer of well-defined composites as 'Solution Building Blocks'. But it's still only *solution*-architecture – the processes that happen *after* we've done the core assessment work for our *enterprise*-architecture.

This isn't trivial. If we can't resolve all the way down to root-primitives – TOGAF's 'Architecture Building Blocks' – we're stuck with the solutions we already have, which may not fit a changed context at all. And if we don't have the right set of primitives at the root-level, we'll be unable to *see* new solutions, or to have any way to rethink what's going on in our enterprise: the taxonomy and ontology define meaning, and hence what is visible, what is deemed 'real' and relevant, and what is not. In his seminars Zachman does take care to portray his framework as covering more than just IT; but most toolset-based implementations of the framework don't – with unfortunate results.

I'm reminded here of a children's-television series of many years ago called *Sapphire and Steel*. In the story, each element was personified as a kind of superhero in a stereotypic war between good and evil. Each character reflected the attributes of its element: Mercury could flow around obstacles, Lead had enormous mass, and so on; "transuranic elements must not be used where life is present", intoned the titles voice-over. However, half the real elements were missing – lack of budget, perhaps? – but the list of 'elements' did include the eponymous Sapphire and Steel. Often wondered how many kids were confused about chemistry as a result of that little bit of artistic licence...

Sapphire and steel are compounds, of course – composites, not primitives. Anyone trying to build a real-world chemistry on the assumption that sapphire and steel are elements is going to come unstuck; and they'll find their options seriously limited if they're missing great chunks of the Periodic Table. But that's pretty much what happens whenever someone tries to do real enterprise-architecture with a conventional IT-centric framework and toolset. Every example I've seen so far is a muddled mixture of composites such as 'Process' or 'IT Application' masquerading as primitives, whilst half the root-primitives we *do* need for whole-of-enterprise architecture – items such as 'physical event', or 'social-network location', or even 'person' – are either in completely inappropriate places in the taxonomy or missing altogether. No wonder it's such a mess...

I'm occasionally accused of fanaticism on this issue, but it really does matter, because our flexibility of options depends on the precision of the metamodel: the closer we can get to true primitives, the more flexibility we have. Most of the time we'll work well above that layer of primitives, but there are a few times – such as planning for disaster-recovery, or for major legislative change – when we really *do* need to get right down to the roots and rethink things from scratch.

Each cell in Zachman's framework represents a class of primitives, whilst composites straddle horizontally across multiple cells of the framework. There are no vertical composites as such: instead, vertical structures such as logical-to-physical data-maps are more accurately trails of derivation or implementation.

The layers in Zachman are usable almost 'as-is' for whole-of-enterprise architecture, because they represent different views and time-frames in the architecture (see *Framework – layers*, p.59). The columns, however, do need much more work to be usable: not only are some of the category-assignments wrong, but in effect there's an entire dimension missing, especially for cells for the lower layers (see *Framework – primitives*, p.63). It's only when we've sorted that out that we have a stable foundation on which to map the layers of composites for solutions – in particular, the intentional 'incompleteness' of components, especially in the higher layers of the framework, which supports their re-use in differing contexts (see *Framework – composites*, p.79).

Entities, properties, relationships and models

The most visible result of the framework is the set of models that many people think of *as* 'architecture'. In essence, though, a model is a description of ideas about the structure of relationships between various types of architectural entities – for example, the 'things' implied by the pigeonholes in the Zachman framework. Each type of model will contain three categories of information:

- *content* – the nouns of the model, providing references to the entities or 'things', such as data-records, or trucks, or business events, or locations, or whatever, sometimes with additional descriptive details of attributes or properties of each entity
- *context* – the adjectives of the model, providing further information or 'metadata' that would place those entities (or the records of those entities) within a broader context, such as the person responsible for that category of entity, or the date and time that the record was last changed
- *connections* – the verbs of the model, providing information about how the entities relate with each other, often literally in the form of a verb such as '‹implements›' or '‹aggregates›'

In a sense, models *are* relationships: each standard model-type provides a standardised means to describe relationships in a structured way. We describe that inner structure of the model-type in a schema or metamodel; in turn, the structure for that would be described by a meta-schema or metametamodel, and so on, in principle ad infinitum. More on this in the chapter on models (see *Framework – models*, p.88).

> The framework is not the architecture, nor are the models the architecture. I know that should be obvious to everyone, but painful experience indicates that it still isn't so for many would-be architects. Time and again we've seen cases where architects have spent many years and many millions of whatever currency in producing a beautiful set of models that are completely useless in practice – and unsurprisingly their clients are not happy about it, or about enterprise architecture in general... Often there's a fair bit of work needed to show that architecture *can* be useful – and the first part of that is to explain what models really do.
>
> An architecture model is a map, a description of some aspect of the business world; but we need to remember that the map is not the territory, and ultimately the territory is what we need to work on, not

> the map. As we saw earlier with business-drivers, the *real* end-product
> of architecture is a dialogue between stakeholders – not a drawing that
> makes sense to architects but probably to no-one else. Ignore this
> point at your peril!

A model exists in a context – how we *use* the model. In conventional IT-architecture, a model is essentially about structure and infrastructure, about relationships between 'things' in a physical or virtual sense. In essence, the aim there is to *engineer* the information technology of the enterprise, viewing every aspect of the IT as a component within a vastly complicated machine. But as we saw earlier (see 'A matter of metaphor' in *Purpose – an overview*, p.22), the idea of 'engineering the enterprise' is fraught with problems at the whole-of-enterprise scale. We need to think more in terms of 'organisation as organism', extending the concept of service-oriented architecture, for example, to the whole-of-enterprise scale with a 'viable services' approach. More on how to model this in practice in the chapter in framework integration – see 'Integration – the service-oriented enterprise' in *Framework – integration*, p.99.

The framework described here is what we use in our own architecture practice, but it is of course just one tool amongst many: do feel free to amend it as you need for your own enterprise.

Application

- What frameworks and other conceptual models do you use to guide your current architecture?
- In what ways have you adapted the underlying metamodels to better describe your enterprise?
- What repositories and toolsets do you use in your enterprise?
- Which frameworks do those toolsets support?

Resources

- Zachman framework: see www.zifa.org
- TOGAF and Zachman: see www.opengroup.org/architecture/togaf8-doc/arch/toc.html (chapter 'ADM and the Zachman Framework')

FRAMEWORK – LAYERS

Summary

For the vertical dimension of the framework, we partition scope in terms of timescale – a set of seven distinct layers or perspectives, from unchanging constants, to items which change moment by moment.

Details

Layers – an overview

If you're familiar with Zachman's framework, its six layers provide us with a starting-point that's essentially as valid in non-IT contexts as in IT-centric ones. The only change we need for whole-of-enterprise architecture is an additional topmost layer, for compatibility with other enterprise standards such as ISO9000.

Strictly speaking, the new layer is a kind of additional dimension, but it's simplest to add it as a row, with a single cell straddling across the columns. This acts as a common space for 'universals' to which *everything* in the enterprise should align: vision, values, core principles, core policies and so on. This 'row zero' represents the core architecture-content discovered during the Preliminary Phase – see *Methodology – preparation*, p.113. All the other rows are split into the respective column-cells, as in the original Zachman. So we end up with a vertical axis like this:

- *Row 0*: '**Universals**' – core constants to which everything should align – identifies the overall region of interest and the key points of connection shared with enterprise partners and other stakeholders
- *Row 1*: '**Scope**' (*Zachman*: 'Planner') – core entities in each category, described in list form, *without* relationships between them - the key 'items of interest' for the enterprise
- *Row 2*: '**Business**' (*Zachman*: 'Owner') – core entities described in more detail, from a business-metrics perspective, including relationships between entities both of the same type ('primitives') and of different types ('composites') - summary form, without attributes for entity-types

- *Row 3*: '**System**' (*Zachman*: 'Designer') – entities expanded out into implementation-*independent* designs - includes descriptive attributes
- *Row 4*: '**Develop**' (*Zachman*: 'Builder') – entities and attributes expanded out into implementation-*dependent* designs, including additional implementations for relationships - for example, cross-reference tables for 'many-to-many' data-relationships
- *Row 5*: '**Implement**' (*Zachman*: 'Sub-contractor' or 'Out of Scope') – implementation of designs into actual software, actual business-processes, work-instructions, hardware, networks etc
- *Row 6*: '**Operations**' (*Zachman*: implied but not described) – individual instances of entities, processes and the like, as created, modified, and acted on in real-time operations

Each row adds another concern or attribute, as follows:

- *Row 0*: constant, unchanging (in principle, at least)
- *Row 1*: adds possibility of change, if usually slowly
- *Row 2*: adds relationships and dependencies between entities
- *Row 3*: adds attributes to abstract 'logical' entities
- *Row 4*: adds details for real-world 'physical' design
- *Row 5*: adds details of intended future deployment
- *Row 6*: adds details of actual (present or past) usage

The rows have a steadily narrowing scope of time, from 'Universals', which, in principle at least, should never change, to 'Operations', which will be changing from moment to moment - in some cases in milliseconds or less. Each row usually represents a different category of responsibility or stakeholder - with senior management responsible for row-0 universals, for example, or strategists at row-1 and -2, architects and solution-designers at row-3 and -4, and line managers and front-line staff at row-5 and -6.

For the architecture-cycle, we need to map the business-question onto the respective layers of the framework (see *Purpose – business-driven architecture*, p.29); likewise for the architectural scope to be covered in the cycle's assessments and solutions (see 'Phase A – establish iteration scope' in *Methodology – assessment*, p.122).

At the uppermost level - the whole-of-enterprise level - we always and only have primitives. As we move down through the layers, it becomes harder to see the primitives that underlie each of the implementation-composites, until at row-6, by definition, *every-*

thing should be an integral component of a composite straddling all of the Zachman columns. There's also a kind of implied boundary between row-3 and row-4 where we shift from abstract design to real-world implementation - a shift that's also marked in management structures by the transition from 'staff' to 'line'.

If we map this to the four dimensions of the tetradian view, the upper levels (rows 0-3) represent the 'Purpose' dimension ('the business'), whilst the lower levels (particularly rows 4-6, but in some ways even upward as far as row-2) increasingly separate out into the three 'People', 'Knowledge' and 'Things' dimensions. The more abstract system-level provides a common integration across the dimensions, particularly as a bridge between rows 3-4.

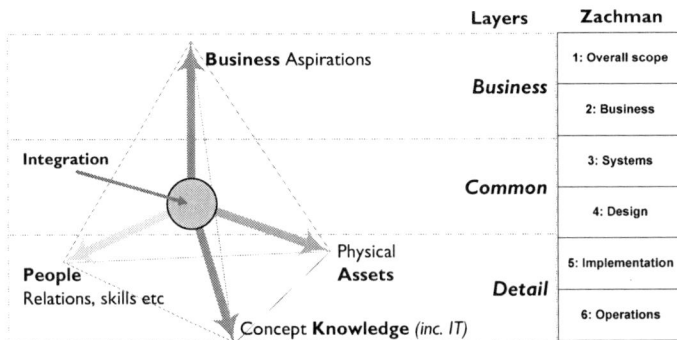

Tetradian dimensions and Zachman rows

More on that dimensional split as we review the Zachman columns in the next chapter - see *Framework - primitives*, p.63.

The boundaries between the meta-layers - business, common and detail - map well to the MDA (Model-Driven Architecture) layers of platform-independent model (PIM) and platform-specific model (PSM). The meta-layers themselves also map well to Phases B to D of the original TOGAF ADM respectively, though there are other reasons why we can't use the meta-layers to drive the methodology for whole-of-enterprise architecture - see 'The architecture cycle' in *Methodology - an overview*, p.108.

Layers – an example

To see how this works in practice, think of the dreaded 'org-chart':

- At *row 0/Universals*, there is just 'the organisation' - the enterprise as a whole.
- At *row 1/Scope*, we could split this into high-level business-units - the basic partitions of the enterprise, as labels for

clusters of overall capabilities (which would be in the row-1 cell for the 'Who ' column) and/or geographic locations (i.e. in the 'Where' column)

- At *row 2/Business*, we would start to differentiate these units, adding labels for the responsible role (the CxO levels) and the relationships between them – and also links to the metrics against which their overall performance would be measured
- At *row 3/System*, we expand out this skeleton into a nested structure of capabilities and reporting-relationships, with at least the upper rows labelled with generic roles and responsibility-types (but not actual names)
- At *row 4/Develop*, we start to become explicit: the upper rows may well start to gain explicit names as well as roles, and every branch needs defined capabilities and responsibilities – but we may use patterns of relationships to indicate lower-level organisational structures that would be re-used at different sites and/or for different capacity-levels (for example, a structure for specific types of work-teams, but without specifying the numbers of work-teams)
- At *row 5/Implement*, we require actual names for every slot in every implemented branch of the organisation-structure – yet this still represents only the *nominal*, intended structure or schedule, not necessarily what happens in practice
- At *row 6/Operations*, we have the real, actual organisation-structure as it changes dynamically day by day, minute by minute, with real-time rosters, with people in 'acting'-roles to cover those on temporary leave, and so on

Application

- In what ways do you partition your current architecture into vertical layers?
- How do you identify and differentiate between these layers?
- How do these layers align with the various business drivers?

Resources

🕸 Zachman framework: see www.zifa.org www
🕸 TOGAF and Zachman layers: see www.opengroup.org/architecture/togaf8-doc/arch/toc.html (chapter 'ADM and the Zachman Framework')

FRAMEWORK – PRIMITIVES

Summary

Below the core-constants, we split the framework horizontally into columns, identifying six distinct major categories of primitives – roughly speaking, what, how, where, who, when and why. In the lower, more implementation-oriented layers of the framework, we also need to split the columns themselves by context into distinct segments or sub-categories – typically related to people, information, things and essential abstracts.

Details

Primitives – an overview

Unlike the Zachman-framework's rows, we really do need to re-think the columns, almost from first-principles, in order to make the framework usable for real enterprise-scope architecture. To understand why, we need to look at a little history.

Way back in the 1980s, Zachman defined just three columns for his original 'framework for information-systems architecture':

- *What* (data)
- *How* (function)
- *Where* (network)

The trouble is that all this gives us is records (data) of actions (function) that happened or should happen somewhere – which in practice is almost meaningless from an enterprise-design perspective. Hence quite early on, Zachman added another three columns:

- *Who* (people)
- *When* (business cycle)
- *Why* (business rule)

All well and good – sort-of. But as soon as we want to move beyond even fairly simple data-and-function modelling, the limitations become apparent. For example, how do we map even basic physical IT-hardware such as servers and routers? They should probably go into the 'What' column – except Zachman says that only holds references to data. Similarly, we can map manual use-cases to the 'Who' column – but there's nowhere to put an automated or IT-based use-case, which we'll need for process re-engineering or service-oriented architecture. Oops...

And there are other, more subtle confusions, too. For example, Zachman correctly asserts that architecture depends on primitives: yet his 'Why' column, he says, consists of 'ends and means'. 'Means' are clearly 'How', not 'Why' – hence 'ends and means' are a composite, not a primitive. As we'll see later, there are other even worse examples of this kind of confusion. So if we use Zachman's framework as-is, we soon find ourselves in a taxonomic black hole – creating real difficulties for design and redesign.

I've seen various attempts to resolve the problems by adding new columns – for 'interface', for example, or 'service'. But in practice, whilst they can seem easier to use for *solutions*-design, at the *architecture* level they make things worse, a further blurring of the crucial boundary between primitives and composites. At the root-level, the framework *must* be composed of true primitives.

So this is a recommended rework for the Zachman columns:

- *What*: **assets** of any kind – physical objects, data, links to people, morale, finances, etc
- *How*: **functions**, activities or services, usually to change something – described independently from the agent (machine, software, person etc) that carries out that activity
- *Where*: **locations** – in physical space (geography etc), virtual space (IP nodes, http addresses etc), relational space (social networks etc) and suchlike
- *Who*: **capabilities** and 'responsibilities', often partitioned into roles, as in the 'actor' of a use-case, or a 'swim-lane' on a process-diagram – which may be human, a machine, a software application, etc, and may be either individual or collective (such as the responsibilities of an organisational unit)
- *When*: **events** and relationships between those events – which may be an event or cycle in time, but might equally be physical (a flood, a system-failure), human (a client initiating a business-process), a trigger from a business-rule (a sensor value, a boundary-condition), and so on
- *Why*: **reasons**, decisions, constraints and other tests which trigger or validate the condition for the 'reason' – as in policy, strategy, business-requirements, business-rules and so on.

The end-result of this rework is that down at the row-5 / Implement level, it should be possible to describe *everything* in terms of a single sentence-structure for work-instructions. This maps to the revised columns as a distinct set of primitives, and as a composite straddling across every column:

"with «*asset*» do «*function*» at «*location*»
using «*capability*» on «*event*» because «*reason*»"

At the row-6/Operations level, the sentence might come out in a slightly different order, and usually in the past tense, but it should still be essentially the same:

"«*function*» was done with «*asset*» by «*capability*»
at «*location*» on «*event*» because «*reason*»"

And although it's a composite, we can still identify the individual component-primitives that make up that composite. Which makes architectural redesign possible, and which anchors the trails of relationships between items and between layers that we need in order to resolve *business*-concerns such as strategic analysis, failure-impact analysis and resolution of complex 'pain-points'.

The other point is that in effect there's an entire *dimension* missing from the Zachman framework, to split each column into distinct and necessary *segments*. As in the examples above, we need to be able to distinguish between physical items, virtual items, people-relationships-as-items; or functions done by machines, by software, by people; and so on.

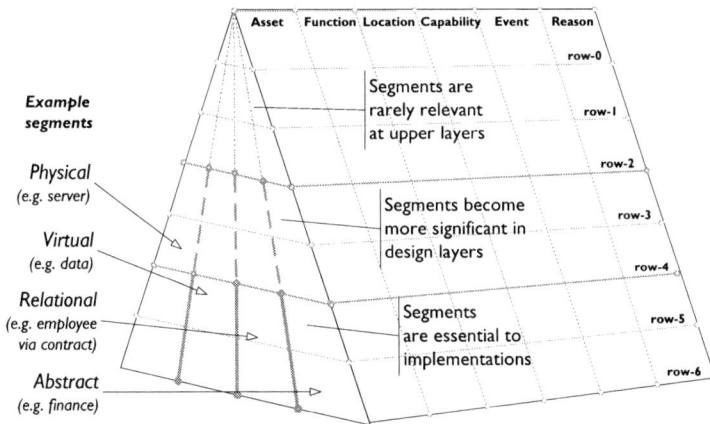

Rows, columns and segments

We'll look at this in more depth as we explore each of the columns in turn.

Assets – 'what?'

Zachman describes the 'What' column as *data*, or more generally as *'entity / relationship'*.

To make this generic enough for enterprise-level architecture, review this column as *'asset'*. Data is just one class of asset – specifically, a *virtual asset*. Architecturally, we need to manage *all* of the assets – not just the data – in a consistent way.

So this column describes the organisation's assets – its countable and measurable 'things' – and the relationships between assets of the same type (as primitives) and different types (as composites). Beyond this expansion to a broader range of assets, and a categorisation into segments of fundamentally different types of assets, the column remains essentially the same as in Zachman.

Segments of the column include:

- *physical assets*: servers, routers, widgets, paper forms, physical objects of all kinds
  - o model types: parts-breakdown, bill of materials, etc
- *virtual assets*: data, metadata, messages, models
  - o model types: data-model, metadata-schema, model-definitions etc
- *relational assets*: links to people – customers, clients, employees and other stakeholders
  - o model types: business-relationships and relationship-types
- *aspirational assets*: morale, values, commitment, drive
  - o model types: architecture 'Universals' (row-zero), customer / employee survey-designs etc
- *abstract assets*: financials, valuations ('goodwill'), energy-resources (electricity, water, network-traffic) etc
  - o model types: financial models, derivatives, valuation schemas etc

The distinctions between the segments are derived from standard classification-schemes for property types. For example, physical property is 'alienable' – if I give a physical object to you, I no longer have it – whereas virtual property is 'non-alienable' – if I give an idea to you, I still have it. And whilst abstract-assets are perhaps the hardest category to understand, they're also the assets about which business is usually most concerned – especially financials.

As an aside, many of our economic problems arise from attempts to treat all property as if it's physical, 'alienable' and controllable – the black farce of 'intellectual property' law being an extreme case in point.

Another common disaster-area is that seemingly well-meant phrase "our people are our greatest asset!". *People* are not assets: it is the *relationship* with each person that is the asset, and needs to be managed as such. Relational assets are the nearest that we get to a true 'Who' in this revised framework - in other words, sort-of 'who' is actually a special class of 'What'.

Within the 'What' column, relationships may exist between primitives of the same segment, or in different segments. Only in the same-segment case – such as the relationships between entities in a data-model – do we have the true primitive-models implied in Zachman's 'entity/relationship' description. All the other cross-segment cases are actually composites, and need to be modelled as such. To say that this can get complicated is an understatement – but we need to be clear about these distinctions if we're to get the architecture to work properly.

An everyday example: a paper form that needs a signature. Sounds straightforward, but architecturally it's a decidedly complex composite.

The form is a physical object: so we need to manage it *as* a physical object, with all of the concomitant complexities of procurement, inventory, pre-use warehousing, modification and use, storage and disposal.

But it also contains data: so we also need to manage it as a virtual asset, with all the concerns about data-quality, information-quality and so on.

Then for something as simple as a signature, we need to identify the relevant role and responsibility ('Who'), link from there back to the specific person allocated that role ('What' – the 'relational asset') to action the respective signature ('How').

And we might well need to record on the form the triggering event ('When'), time and place ('Where') and business-rule ('Why') for the signature.

Much more complex than it seems at first sight, then.

So what? you might say. The answer is that as long as nothing changes, this kind of analysis is indeed irrelevant – an 'academic exercise'. But the moment we want to change something, it becomes essential to split the composite into its primitives, and assess each in turn so as to improve overall effectiveness.

For example, if you want to eliminate all the physical messiness of a paper form, and turn it into pure virtual data, you must also re-think the process of sign-off: otherwise what you'll end up with is the virtual record and *another* paper form, which you now somehow have to synchronise – not only defeating the object of the exercise, but actually making it worse from a maintenance point of view. And when you *do* change to a virtual sign-off, you should also be able to automate links to the 'When', the 'Where' and the 'Why' – they don't need to be left on the online form to be manually filled-in every time, as I saw happening on a system design at a recent client! Unless we can split the composite into its primitives, these issues and options remain invisible - hiding real risks or opportunities for improvement.

To summarise, the 'What' column represents the *assets* of the enterprise – the entities that actions are done with, or to, in the pursuit of the enterprise's business-purpose.

Functions – 'how?'

Zachman describes this as 'process / input-output'. This again is misleading: a process is a sequence of such transforms, a *path* through a set of functions threaded together in a meaningful way with events, data, objects and do on – and is thus a composite, not a primitive. The true primitive here is *function*, in the mathematical sense – in other words something is changed between input and output, as $a=func(x,y)$ and suchlike.

The list of inputs consist of two distinct types: the item(s) to be transformed; and the catalyst(s) which trigger or guide the transformation without themselves being changed.

The activity of the function proper marshals the inputs, changes the state or condition of the items to be transformed, puts the changed items and the catalysts back into their proper places, records the results as required, and signals that the function is complete. For example:

- a low-level software function retrieves its attributes from the stack, carries out the required transforms and other activities, then places its results on the stack for the next function
- a technician selects a casting to machine, configures up a lathe with a set of tools and settings, carries out the required transforms, puts away the machine-tools, amends the work-record, and places the machined casting into the output tray for the next operator to carry out the next stage.

In each case there's also an internal decision to identify that the transform is complete.

Since functions act on things - How acts on What - the segments should be much the same as for the What column:

- *physical*: transform physical objects
- *virtual*: transform data
- *relational*: transform business-relationships - for example, to close a sale
- *abstract*: transform financials - for example, financial derivatives

> In principle there are also functions that operate on aspirational assets such as morale and values, but they're so little understood – especially in large organisations – that it's simplest to skip them for now. Aspirational assets are important, though, as catalyst-inputs to relational functions.

As with the What column, these are distinct segments: for example, on its own, a software function will not change a physical object or a business relationship. But we can transform across segments via composites: software can change physical objects through an NC machine-tool, data supports changes in customer-relationships in a call-centre business-function, and so on.

Typical model-types are the classic functional-decompositions: a high-level function decomposes to low-level sub-processes which include subsidiary functions. The only complication here is that it's not a straightforward primitive-to-primitive decomposition, as it is with a parts-breakdown, for example: a function (primitive) often decomposes to a set of processes (composites) which contain functions (primitives).

For architectural purposes it's important to separate out the primitive function (How) not just from its surrounding inputs and outputs (What) and events (When), but also from the capabilities and responsibilities (Who) that enable the function. If we don't do this, we end up with a blurred composite masquerading as a primitive – in other words, a future roadblock to change or improved effectiveness. This blurring is reflected in the history of software engineering:

- *procedural programming*: centred on function (How), but merged with capability (Who), data (What) and business-rules (Why)
- *object-oriented programming*: centred on data (What), with attached function, and again often with merged capability and business-rules
- *service-oriented architecture*: centred on function, usually without merged data and business-rules, but often with merged capability - i.e. implied or assumed

The ideal for service-oriented architecture is to show the linkages to capability, data and business-rules, but still keep everything separate and distinct. More on that when we look at the Who column.

Locations – 'where?'

Zachman describes this as 'node / link', and "the locations relevant to the organisation" – which is fair enough as long as we expand the meaning of 'node', 'location' and 'link' to cover the broader range of 'What'-type segments:

- *physical*: geographic locations, building/room-numbers and other physical locations
  - o model-types: logistics maps, schematics, map-coordinates, etc
- *virtual*: network locations, IP addresses, web-addresses, Java-style code-addresses, telephone numbers
  - o model-types: network-maps, network-coordinates, number-allocation maps, address-hierarchies, file-hierarchies etc
- *relational*: relative locations for people
  - o model-types: social-network maps, reporting-relationship matrices, etc
- *aspirational* and/or *abstract*: value-webs, dependencies
  - o model-types: Porter value-chains, dependency-trails, audit-trails, etc
- *abstract*: temporal locations, etc
  - o model-types: timelines, project timescales, etc

> Note that time is, in effect, a type of Where – not When – because whilst When-events may happen *in* time, time *itself* is not an event. Likewise, time is not an asset, a What – it does not belong to the enterprise, and there's nothing that the enterprise can do to change it!

As with the How column, we'll often find composites across the segments, for example:

- IT network map, showing both physical and virtual relationships of servers, routers etc
- organisation/region map, showing physical and relational locations of key staff or business units
- logistics value-web map, showing physical and value-step (aspirational/abstract) locations in multi-partner value-chains

In any case, we'll usually find 'Where' as part of a complex composite with What, How and other columns, for example:

- *org-chart*: role (Who) plus relationships (Where » relational); sometimes geographic location (Where » physical), also actual person (What » relational)
- *full IT-network map*: physical (Where » physical) and IP addresses (Where » virtual) of servers, routers etc, with hardware IDs (What » physical) and roles (Who » relational) or persons (What » relational) responsible for their maintenance, and identifiers for the applications (How » virtual) that run on them

As before, we need to be able to separate out the Where primitives from the others in the composites as required, for architectural re-use of the same patterns elsewhere.

The 'link' relationships of the primitive are fairly straightforward. As we move downward through the Zachman rows, we can create the same kind of expanding decompositions as for What, without the primitive-to-composite complications we met in the How column.

Not hard, anyway. The item *at* a location is usually some kind of What, and hence usually making some kind of composite with Where; but the primitive Where is *location* – in whatever form that location might take.

Capabilities – 'who?'

From my experience, this is one place where Zachman made a serious mistake in his taxonomy, and has kept on compounding the resultant problems ever since.

The 'Who' label sort-of fits, and gives a nice symmetry, of course; but describing the content as *'people'* – as Zachman does – is dangerously misleading. The actual content is closer to 'Which', or closer again to 'By Whom' or even 'By What', because what's needed as the primitive here is *capabilities*, usually clustered into sets as **roles** and their *responsibilities*. The catch is that the role is still abstract: to bring it to life, so to speak, it needs to be linked in a composite with an appropriate 'What' – in other words as the *agent*, a term that Zachman does occasionally use for this column.

The point is that the agent can be anything active: the 'What' for the composite with 'Who' may be a person (relational), but it might equally be a machine (physical) or a software application (virtual). Linking an agent (Who plus What) to a function (How) is what makes a process possible – as indicated, for example, by the swimlanes in a BPMN process-model, or the actor and use-case in a UML use-case model.

In order to model abstract-services, or the complex trade-offs between manual, machine and IT-based services required for process reengineering, we need to keep the functions (How) distinct from the capabilities (Who), and the capabilities separate and distinct from any implementation (What) for those capabilities. So describing the content of this column as 'Who' – or worse, as 'people' – creates a huge risk of confusion, by bundling together a composite of distinct primitives (Who plus What) into a kind of 'pseudo-primitive' of the agent – and only human agents at that. Worse again, in the most common variant of the framework, Zachman compounds the difficulties by describing the primitive here as 'relationships between people and work' – which is actually a muddled composite of any combination of Who, What»relational and How. So although – for sanity's sake – we're best to leave the column-label unchanged, as 'Who', we do need to keep reminding ourselves regularly as to what it really represents.

The segment definitions here are less easy to define: the boundaries seem a bit blurred whichever way we cut them. It's easy to see that specific capabilities apply to the physical, virtual and relational domains from the What and How columns, for example; but most real-world roles – clusters of capabilities – require a combination across these segments. Perhaps a better cut, which does map indirectly to What and How but rather more closely to Why, is on what we might call skill-levels, drawn in part from the Cynefin model of organisational complexity:

- *rule-based* (Cynefin 'known' domain; aligns with *physical* segments): no choice or judgement permitted, hence little to no true skill (i.e. training only); real-time or near-real-time only, and strictly causal; may be implemented by machines, IT or people (the latter usually under protest, from incipient boredom!)
- *analytic* (Cynefin 'knowable' domain; aligns with *virtual* segments): some judgement required, with choices amongst variously complicated paths, which may include delays and disconnects in time, but still modelled in terms of assumed cause-effect relationships; usually cannot be implemented by machines without IT-based or human support
- *heuristic* (Cynefin 'complex' domain; aligns with *relational* segments): true skills, judgement always required – 'probe /

sense / respond', in Cynefin terms – to assess patterns in contexts with high uncertainties, limited statistical probabilities, complex delay-loops and/or unknown or unidentified factors; apparent cause-effect patterns may only be identified retrospectively; cannot be implemented by machines or conventional IT-based systems without human support

- *principle-based* (Cynefin 'chaotic' domain; aligns with *aspirational* and/or *abstract* segments): very high skill-levels, extreme and inherent uncertainty in real-time or near-real-time; no direct cause-effect patterns identifiable (e.g. 'market of one'); can only be implemented by humans

The key advantage of this cut is that it clarifies the kinds of What can be combined with a Who capability-set to create the respective agent. Trying to set up an IT system to implement principle-based capabilities is asking for trouble, for example, though too many system-designs that I've seen over the years have implicitly made that mistake... It also helps in clarifying the difference between responsibility in the sense of agency, and responsibility in the sense of *accountability* – because action and oversight often require different skill-levels for the same nominal business-function.

Right now there's no obvious notation that can be used for modelling the many-to-many relationships between capabilities and roles. The nearest equivalent would be data entity relationship diagrams, with roles as entities and capabilities as attributes; but that doesn't quite capture the semantic independence of the capabilities themselves, nor the implied skill-levels.

To summarise, the appropriate primitive for the Who column is not 'people', as in the original Zachman, but *capability*, usually linked with other capabilities into one or more abstract **roles**.

Events – 'when?'

Zachman describes the 'When' column as *'Time / cycle'*, but it's like labelling 'Who' as *'People'* – it seems common-sense, but unfortunately it's subtly and dangerously wrong for the taxonomy. The appropriate primitive here is the more generic term *'event'*, and relationships between these events. Time is usually an *attribute* of an event, but not necessarily *is* the event itself; it's just one of several categories or segments of events, and 'cycle' is only one of several types of relationship between time-events.

The Business Process Modelling Notation specification gives some useful pointers to the probable segments here: it lists message-events, timer-events, business-rule events and so on. Missing from that list are physical events and relational (people) events – not surprising, though, since the BPMN specification is strongly IT-oriented. For the segments, it's probably simplest to use the same set as for the 'What' column:

- *physical events*: includes 'disaster' incidents - fire, flood etc - and any other kind of physical trigger-event
- *virtual events*: includes messages and other data-triggers
- *relational events*: includes meetings, phone-contacts, sign-offs and other people-based trigger-events
- *aspirational events*: includes business-rules (because these focus on meaning and purpose)
- *abstract events*: includes time-based triggers, business-cycles and the like

Relationships between events will often be nested and hierarchical: for example, cycles may contain smaller cycles, and so on ad infinitum. Other relationships may be chained, as in a project Gantt chart.

As with other columns, we'll often find event-primitives that link into composites across the column segments: an out-of-range data-value triggers a business-rule which triggers a virtual message; likewise a message may arise from a mechanical sensor, or the sign-off of a document. So there's some juggling of primitives and composites that we may need to do here; but the basic principle seems sound. The only complication is that, by definition, responses to events are reactive: if we want the enterprise to become more proactive, we need to create an architectural context in which at least some of the events are future-focussed.

> Somewhat confusing, given the 'When' column-heading, but we need to remember that time itself is actually a *location* – a coordinate or 'Where'. A marker on the time-coordinate can be a source of an Event (the taxonomy content for 'When') but is not itself the primary content for the 'When' column.
>
> As mentioned earlier, it's possible to argue that time is an asset – a 'What' – but that doesn't really work either: agreed, it's sort-of a measurable 'thing', but it's not directly owned by or linked to the enterprise as assets are. Describing time as a coordinate is more useful, and probably more accurate, not least because given a trajectory – i.e. a function or 'How', based on a rule, a 'Why' – we can calculate location in time from physical position, and vice-versa.

Anyway, the summary: the primitives for the When column are *events*, and relationships such as cycles which provide meaningful links between those events.

Reasons – 'why?'

Zachman describes this column as 'motivation', and defines the primitive as 'ends / means'. That definition gives us problems straight away, because it's another pseudo-primitive: not 'Why' on its own, but a composite of Why ('ends') and How ('means'). A more appropriate primitive here is *decision*, linked together in webs and trails of derivations that ultimately anchor back to '*the* decision', the enterprise Vision. Decisions and similar 'reasonings' underpin motivation, so Zachman's overall description for the column would still be valid.

Another reason for changing the definition of the primitive here is that we need a broader scope than 'business rules' - Zachman's only example at the mid to lower levels. Business rules, requirements, constraints, policies, analyses, all the other decisions that underpin strategy and tactics - these are the *reasons* we do anything in the enterprise, and are what we need to document in the Why column.

As with Who, there are several ways we could cut the segments, but perhaps the most useful is the Cynefin set, indicating the degree of flexibility (or lack of it, as 'bindedness') in the decision:

- *rule-based* (Cynefin 'known' domain; aligns somewhat with *physical* segments): 'law', mandatory, no flexibility – must always link to source(s) that justify the rigidity of the decision, such as analytics, external legislation, etc
- *analytic* (Cynefin 'knowable' domain; aligns somewhat with *virtual* segments): 'best-practice' decision depends on multiple factors and/or transforms – should be linked to the factors (What), transforms (How) etc on which it is based, and to sources for standards
- *heuristic* (Cynefin 'complex' domain; aligns somewhat with *relational* segments): contextual guidelines – should link to other decisions or items identifying the context, and to roles or persons responsible for maintenance of the guidelines
- *principle-based* (Cynefin 'chaotic' domain; aligns somewhat with *aspirational* and/or *abstract* segments): decision derived from high level of skill – must link to guiding principles and to person or group (e.g. committee) responsible for the decision

This also matches the layering of source-documents in ISO-9000: rule-based *work-instructions* derive from analytic or best-practice *procedures* derived from heuristic *policies* or guidelines, derived in turn from the principles indicated by the *vision*.

> Incidentally, that trajectory-calculation described in the When column also illustrates well the different categories of 'Decision' in the Why column. In a simplistic school-level version of a Newtonian world the location-versus-time calculation is a single-factor *rule-based* function; in a more realistic version of Newtonian physics there are many more *analytic* factors that need to be taken into account, such as wind-speed, the rotation of the earth and so on; at quantum levels we're more reliant on *heuristics* and patterns to guide the estimate; whilst in a truly chaotic world we would rely on *principles*, or perhaps prayer!

Typical model-types include requirements methodologies such as Volere, and strategy/tactics models such as the Business Motivation Model – though note that the latter's concept of 'vision' is simply a view of a 'desirable future state' for short-term strategy, rather than the invariant Vision required in row-zero to guide and anchor principle-based decisions.

Relationships between reasons include '‹expands on›' (especially when descending down the Zachman rows) and 'conflicts with'. The other columns will usually include extensive cross-links to the Why column, with relationships such as '‹implements›' (for example, How or What implements decision). Every requirement also needs links to one or more items – usually What or How – that provide a test to confirm when the requirement has been met.

In principle, *every* relationship between any items in the entire framework is also a decision, and thus technically should belong in the Why column. In effect, a relationship is a special type of decision that links two other items together. The same Cynefin types would apply to these as to other decisions: some relationships, such as foreign-key links in a database schema, are rule-based; others, such as assignments of people (What»virtual) to roles (Who»virtual) to business functions (How) are more likely to be based on best-practice or guidelines; and so on. For clarity, and for sanity's sake, we display these decisions as connecting lines rather than as Zachman entities: but at times we need to remember that that *is* what they are.

To summarise: the primitives for the amended Why column are decisions and other given *reasons*, with specific relationships such as 'expands on' and 'conflicts with' to link them together into a single tree ultimately anchored in the enterprise Vision.

Synopsis

To summarise this overall review of the Zachman framework, the *columns* or content-types and primitive-types:

- *What*: **assets** of any kind – physical objects, data, links to people, morale, finances, etc
- *How*: **functions** – activities or services to create change, described independently from the agent (machine, software, person etc) that carries out that activity
- *Where*: **locations** – in physical space (geography etc), virtual space (IP nodes, http addresses etc), relational space (social networks etc), time and suchlike
- *Who*: **capabilities** clustered as **roles** – may be human, machine, software application, etc, and individual or collective
- *When*: **events** – may be in time, or physical, virtual, human or other event
- *Why*: **reasons** – decisions, constraints and the like, as in strategy, policy, business-requirements, business-rules, regulations etc.

The *segments* or sub-categories within the columns: could be cut multiple ways, but typically:

- **physical**: tangible objects (What), mechanical processes (How), physical or temporal locations (Where), physical events (When); also align to *rule-based* skills (Who) and decisions (Why)
- **virtual**: intangible objects such as data (What), software processes (How), logical locations (Where), data-driven events (When); also align to *analytic* skills (Who) and decisions (Why)
- **relational**: links to people (What), manual processes (How), social/relational locations (Where), human events (When); also align to *heuristic* skills (Who) and decisions (Why)
- **aspirational**: principles and values (What), value-webs and dependencies (Where), business-rules (When); also align with *principle-based* skills (Who) and decisions (Why)
- **abstract**: additional uncategorised segments such as financial (What, How), energy (What) etc

Application

- What do you recognise as a 'primitive' in an architectural sense?
- How do you distinguish between primitives and composites?
- If you use an EA toolset, what primitives does it support?
- How does it structure those primitives and their relationships with each other? – i.e. what taxonomy does it use?
- What means – if any – does it provide to separate out primitives from the composites and other 'solution building blocks'?
- As you expand the scope of your architecture, which primitives are missing from your toolset's taxonomy?
- How do you identify that those primitives *are* missing from the taxonomy?
- What means – if any – does your toolset provide to extend its taxonomies and metamodels with definitions for new primitives, composites and relationships?

Resources

- Zachman framework: see www.zifa.org
- TOGAF and Zachman primitives: see www.opengroup.org/architecture/togaf8-doc/arch/toc.html (chapter 'ADM and the Zachman Framework')
- BPMN (Business Process Modelling Notation): see www.bpmn.org
- UML (Unified Modelling Language) use-case notation: see www.agilemodeling.com/artifacts/useCaseDiagram.htm
- Cynefin model of organisational complexity: see en.wikipedia.org/wiki/Cynefin and www.cognitive-edge.com
- ISO9000:2000: see en.wikipedia.org/wiki/ISO_9000
- Volere requirements methodology: see www.volere.co.uk/
- Business Motivation Model: see www.businessrulesgroup.org/bmm.shtml

FRAMEWORK – COMPOSITES

Summary

Architectural primitives are often of little value on their own: to be usable, they need to be linked together into composites which represent some real-world entity or pattern. Composites will often be layered into more complex entities, moving towards a description that is complete enough to use in practice.

Details

Composites – an overview

Primitives are the building-blocks for the architecture, but on their own they're usually of little real use. In the real world, very few of the 'things' we deal with are simple enough to be handled as true primitives – data being one of the few examples that is, which might be why there's so much emphasis on data in conventional 'enterprise'-architecture… For the rest, we usually won't see the primitives as such, unless we choose to do so for architectural reasons; instead, they're more likely to be bundled together into *composites* that bridge across the Zachman columns and segments – compound entities that we can treat as a single unit.

Composites are the basis for solution-designs. A reference framework such as the TOGAF 'Integrated Information Infrastructure Reference Model' will consist almost entirely of standardised composites to be used in solution-designs.

Composites will also often be layered, in several different senses. One is that although a composite will usually straddle columns and segments only within a single Zachman layer, similar *types* of composites do often appear in different layers. Lower-layer composites also derive from or expand on those at higher levels – for example:

- *data*: correspondences and mappings between 'logical' (row-3) and 'physical' (row-4) data-models
- *process*: high-level abstract process (row-3) decomposes to detailed lower-level service-patterns (row-4) and to work-instructions (row-5)

- *org-chart*: abstract pattern of reporting-relationships repeats in similar ways from conceptual layer (row-2) all the way down to real-time operations (row-6)
- *requirements-tree*: abstract-pattern of derivations repeats and expands outward from layer to layer

Another kind of layering is that composites will themselves be bundled together to form more complex composites. A database server would be a good example of this: it will include a software server-application (a bundling of *function* and *capability*) and a defined set of data (a virtual *asset*), maintained within a computer system (a physical *asset*) running a specific operating system and the like (further bundlings of *function* and *capability*) at a specific network address (a combination of virtual and physical *location*). For many design purposes it's useful to treat the whole composite server as a single unit; but for some redesigns we may need to 'unbundle' it in a wide variety of ways to view its sub-composites, and thence to change its operating-system, for example, or host-machine, or network rack-location, or whatever.

As we work downward through the Zachman layers towards real-world implementation, we aggregate primitives and simpler composites into ever-larger and more complex composites, until finally, at the operations layer, *everything* is or is part of a composite that straddles every framework column.

> Though not necessarily every segment of that column, of course. A service, for example, is a composite of *function* and *capability* that could be implemented by almost any combination of manual-process (i.e. relational segments), IT-process (virtual segments) or machine-process (physical segments) – but usually not all of them at once!

In the same way, whenever we want to redesign something – often, but not always, moving up through the Zachman layers to do so – we'll need to disaggregate the composites back into their simpler sub-composites and, on occasion, right back to primitives. Composites are always closer to the real world, and often easier to understand, but also constrain the possibilities for redesign: getting the balance of abstractions right is one of the subtler arts of architecture…

Another reason we might want to disaggregate composites is to identify scope for an architecture iteration. We work backwards from composites to their underlying primitives, to give us a set of framework cells that are covered by the context. One reason for doing this is to provide clues as to what else might be affected by the context of the architecture iteration – see 'Phase A – establish iteration scope' in *Methodology – assessment*, p.122.

But the key point in all of this is Zachman's aphorism that architecture is about primitives, whilst design is about composites. The moment we want to *do* something, we need to be able to plug the components of our architecture together into things we can use in practice. So we need to be able to *think* in terms of primitives, but composites are what we *use*; that's the fundamental difference.

Root-composites

At the root-level we have what may seem at first to be the same as architectural primitives, but are actually primitive building-blocks for *solutions*, not architecture. The difference is critical, because as we saw with earlier with some of Zachman's original columns, if we use these root-composites *as* architectural primitives, we end up being unable to see other opportunities for redesign, or ways out of disaster-recovery problems, and so on.

> Remember *Sapphire and Steel* (p.56)? It's in down-to-the-roots redesigns for assumption-challenging issues such as disaster-recovery that mistaking composites for primitives really starts to hurt. The simple rule is that if you can split it, either across columns, or across segments, then it's a composite, not a primitive.
>
> Perhaps the easiest way to remember this is that if architectural primitives are atoms, root-composites are the lowest-level molecules or ions – water being the obvious example, as H_2O or the radicals OH– and H+. As in architecture, many atom-level substances only appear in nature as members of composites: primitive-hydrogen and -oxygen don't like being alone, so to speak, and usually occur in nature as the composites H_2 and O_2 – which reminds us, too, that composites aren't always heterogeneous compounds. Gold, Au, is one of the minority that does occur on its own, but it doesn't like mixing with anything else, either – though that has its uses too, of course…
>
> We could play with this metaphor quite a long way, but it's probably more useful to get back to architecture!

It's sometimes useful to think of root-composites as 'pseudo-primitives'; but even that can be misleading at times, because in a sense they *are* the primitives for solution-designs in some chosen context. Just not for architecture, which needs to be as 'context-free' as possible at the whole-enterprise scale.

We'll often come across variants of Zachman that try to 'bring it up to date' by adding extra columns for 'service' or 'interface' or the like. As we saw earlier, treating such composites as primitives would be a disastrous mistake at the architectural level; but for *solution*-design it's actually a good idea. Depending on the busi-

ness context, it's well worth while creating one or more frameworks or structures as a guide for solution-architecture – using
Zachman layering, perhaps, together with your own choice of
columns based on appropriate root-composites such as service
and interface.

It doesn't have to be a Zachman-like framework, of course. In this
regard, one of the odder losses in recent years has been the virtual
disappearance of Troux Metis' *Metis Enterprise Architecture Framework*
(MEAF). Somewhat IT-centric, of course, but much less so than usual –
though apparently Disney complained that there was no built-in entity
for 'theme-park'! Beyond the absence of that apparently essential item,
it provided an excellent selection of real-world 'things' and other
design-level root-composites, clustered into about thirty different
'domains' such as Analysis, Financial, IT Architecture, Location, Policy,
Product and Service.

It was based on a very good metamodel and the like, which gave the
framework a great deal of strength and flexibility. But what it *didn't*
have, unfortunately, was a proper framework of real primitives behind
it – hence no built-in way to handle Disney's complaint, other than to
create yet another not-quite-primitive root-composite. But it was a
great framework for solution-level analysis and solution-design: worth
looking out for if you can find it.

Anything goes, really, as long as we remember that such frameworks – and the higher-level 'reference frameworks' we build
upon them – are simply an aid to design: and in design, what
matters is what works, not whether it's academically 'pure' or
suchlike. We just need to be careful not to confuse them with the
real primitives-framework that we'll need when we do have go
right down to the roots of the architecture.

Some example root-composites

- network node – bundle of virtual and physical *location*, often
  implicitly or explicitly linked to a physical *asset* such as a
  router or server
- machine (such as a server or photocopier) – bundles *capability*
  (physical and/or virtual) into a physical *asset*
- application – bundle of *capabilities* and, often, explicitly-
  defined virtual *functions*, also often explicitly linked to specific
  virtual *assets* (data)
- metric – bundle of virtual *asset* (data) and the virtual *functions*
  and *capabilities* to derive business-meaning from that data
- business unit – cluster of *capabilities* and *functions* at a distinct
  physical (geographic) and/or relational (hierarchic) *location*

- responsibility – cluster of *capabilities* and *decisions* that may be assigned to any active *asset* and/or *function*
- user – bundle of *capabilities* and/or *functions* associated with an *asset* that may be relational (i.e. link to a real person), virtual (e.g. 'consumer' software-service) or even physical (e.g. next unit in an automated assembly-line)

> For solution-design purposes you might also include 'Person' or 'Party' as a root-composite - but If you do so, remember that warning earlier (see p.67) that people are not assets!
>
> As with Zachman's original 'Who' column-heading, 'Person' is a useful shorthand way to describe a clustering of capabilities and responsibilities and the like, but such clusterings are not necessarily linked to any real person – a key point in process-redesign. And it's essential to remember that they can be linked to a real person *only* via a business-relationship: if the relationship is weakened or lost, so is the link with the person – which means the capability is lost, too. Bye-bye business-process, in fact.
>
> Making each of these relationships explicit can at first seem a tedious discipline, but it pays off handsomely in complex issues such as business-process redesign and disaster-recovery – and also in reducing potential problems with disgruntled people who understandably don't like being referred to as 'assets'…

Complex composites

As we move closer to the real world, the composites tend to get more complex. They often extend across more columns – 'process' being the obvious example, which typically covers *event, capability, function, asset* and a subset of *decision*. In other cases, particularly in the row-3 'logical' layer, they'll oscillate between an abstract entity that's almost a primitive, and one of several more-concrete entities that expand out to specific implementations in different segments of the primitive.

> That'll no doubt sound way too abstract at first, so here's a real example, which comes from one of our assignments with a large logistics organisation.
>
> Our initial brief was to create a Functional Business Model of the small-packet logistics operation – but to do so in *functional* terms, deliberately playing down the details of how each function was implemented. In effect, each 'function' was a root-composite, placed in one of four layers, almost equivalent to the Zachman row-1 to row-4. In the upper layers, implementation was almost irrelevant: all we needed there were the metrics, the KPIs and so on.
>
> Down at the row-4 level, we were obviously concerned about differences between, say, sorting packets by hand, by machine, or pre-sorted via IT – in framework terms, different implementations in,

respectively, the *relational, physical* and *virtual* segments of the *function* column. But at the row-3 level, the 'logical' layer where most of the initial stages for redesigns take place, we kind of oscillate between ignoring implementation – in order to understand how packet-sorting, in this example, fits within the bigger picture – and wanting to know those implementation details – so we can understand the various trade-offs. So the composite for the process needs to be both detailed *and* not-detailed, at the same time. The abstract entity *encapsulates* the concrete, parallel implementations; the whole thing is, in effect, a single complex composite.

There are also sort-of composites that form patterns both within and between framework layers. An obvious example in data-architecture is the many-to-many relationship in relational database design: at the row-3 'logical' layer this would be shown as two tables with a single relationship between them, and in the row-4 'physical' layer as slightly-expanded versions of the same two tables with an extra table between them to carry the required cross-reference records. The cross-reference table is thus an *implementation pattern*, and also a pattern of relationships between the layers.

Other patterns 'decompose' at different layers, often expanding outward in a kind of hierarchy, gaining more implementation-detail as they downward towards the real world, but still retaining a similar overall pattern of structure and interrelationships. A layered parts-breakdown is one such example; a tree of requirements is another; an org-chart yet another; likewise a work breakdown structure for a project-plan. Another hierarchical pattern, the 'viable systems model', provides one of the best ways to understand organisational structure at the whole-of-enterprise level, as we'll see later (see 'Integration – the service-oriented enterprise' in *Framework – integration*, p.99). Hierarchical patterns of this kind are some of the most valuable we can find, because they greatly simplify not just the design but the *comprehensibility* of complex systems: so it's well worth developing an eye for such things as you explore and develop your enterprise architecture.

Much the same applies to patterns in general: a common definition is that they are "a way of capturing architectural design ideas as archetypal and re-usable descriptions", which should tell us straight away that they're composites for solution-designs. Christopher Alexander's original work on patterns was aimed at physical architecture – 'towns, buildings, construction', to quote the subtitle of his much-referenced book – but in practice, and with a bit of metaphoric tweaking, they apply just as well in software design, in process-flows and much else besides. There are plenty of pattern resources around on the net, such as the well-known Portland Pattern Repository: they're all worth exploring as potential sources for composites – or, at the least, ideas for composites – that you can use and re-use in your own architectural work.

The other key point about composites is the concept of 'completeness', in an architectural sense – but we'll come back to that in a moment.

Some example complex-composites

- design-pattern (abstract software process, abstract business-process, 'business-object' data-structure etc)
- business process – layered decomposition of *event*, responsibility / role (complex of *capability*, *decision* and *asset*), *function*, *decision* and *asset*
- value-chain – layered decomposition of business-process and abstract *asset/decision* composite ('value')
- organisation-structure – layered decomposition of *location*, *capability*, *function* and *asset*
- strategy – layered decomposition of *decision* ('ends') and *capability* and/or *function* ('means')

Composites and 'completeness'

As we move down the framework rows, we also move more towards a kind of architectural 'completion' – towards something we can actually *use*. As we saw in the discussion on primitives, by the time we get down to row-5, we need a composite that covers every column of the framework: "with «*asset*» do «*function*» at «*location*» using «*capability*» on «*event*» because «*reason*»". More to the point, if any column is missing, the process – or whatever it is – won't work: it *needs* to be complete.

But if it's complete, we can't change anything. The whole idea of abstraction is to allow substitution, replacement, re-design. So if we describe an actor in a business process in terms of a role rather than a specific person, then that task could be done by *anyone* with the appropriate skills and experience – or perhaps by a machine, if the task can be simplified down to that level. If we design a business-process, but intentionally don't specify *where* the process is to be used, it can be done in any location (in theory, at least, if not necessarily in practice). In software, a variable parameter is a 'placeholder' that we deliberately leave incomplete, to be filled in at run-time; the same for a database schema, which specifies how a database record is to be structured, but not the exact details of what it contains. Which brings us to an important principle:

Composites are usable to the extent that they're architecturally complete;
composites are *re*-usable to the extent that they're architecturally *in*complete

> Not exactly a new idea, of course: the Chinese philosopher Lao Tsu described much the same notion well over two thousand years ago in the classic *Tao Te Ching,*, if in rather more poetic form:
>
> Thirty spokes share the wheel's hub;
>   it is the centre hole that makes it useful.
> Shape clay into a vessel;
>   it is the space within that makes it useful.
> Cut doors and windows for a room;
>   it is the holes which make it useful.
> Therefore profit comes from what is there;
>   usefulness from what is not there.
>
> Lao Tsu could almost be described as the world's first whole-of-enterprise architect – where 'enterprise' in that case was an entire empire! Although the details of the context are different, the *Tao* is certainly worth perusing with a present-day architect's eye – especially in a good translation such as that by Gia Fu Feng above.

Another type of incompletion is what we might call 'bindedness' – the extent to which a particular item must be included or applied within a solution. The obvious example is legislative compliance - because if we don't comply, we're breaking the law – but it also applies to other practical concerns such as whether a particular operating-system or software version or model of plastics moulding machine should be used, and for what purposes; or what types of skills and experience are needed in order to deliver a particular service or decision. The levels of bindedness for any item – composite or primitive – would include:

- *mandatory*: item must be used wherever appropriate
- *recommended*: item should be used unless a preferred solution mandates an alternative
- *desirable*: use of the item would aid in consistency
- *suggested*: experience indicates the item may provide a better or more consistent solution than similar alternatives

> There's a useful parallel here with the the MoSCoW priorities for business-requirements – Must, Should, Could, can Wait – and also with the Cynefin domains – rule-based, analysis for best-practice, heuristic guidelines, and principles.

This is the basis of a Technical Reference Model and the like: it's a reference-model *because* it's deemed to be binding in some way. It's also how we specify which Standards should be used, in what contexts, and for what purposes. More on this later when we look at the assessment phases of the methodology – see *Methodology – assessment*, p.121 – and the process of managing architecture 'dispensations' – see 'Phase G – guide implementation' in *Methodology – solutions*, p.153, and also *Methodology – hands-off architecture*, p.161.

Application

- What patterns and other composites are defined for your existing architecture models?
- What reference-models of composites do you use within the architecture for your specific enterprise? What scope – enterprise, industry, technology, etc – is covered by each of these reference-models? What is the 'bindedness' of each? How do you resolve overlaps and layering between reference-models?
- To what extent are composites within those models treated as or confused with true primitives (as pseudo-primitives)?
- What layering of composites is supported? How are relationships between the layers traced?
- What support – if any – does your existing architecture toolset provide for links between entities in different layers?
- What processes exist within your architecture practice to derive composites and primitives (abstraction) and to derive solutions from composites (linkage and specialisation)?

Resources

- TOGAF ABBs, SBBs and Enterprise Continuum: see www.opengroup.org/architecture/togaf8-doc/arch/toc.html (chapter 'Introduction to the Enterprise Continuum' and following)
- Portland Pattern Repository: see www.c2.com/cgi/wiki?PatternIndex
- Human/Computer Interface Pattern-Form Gallery: see www.cs.kent.ac.uk/people/staff/saf/patterns/gallery.html
- Christopher Alexander, *A Pattern Language: towns, buildings, construction* (Oxford University Press, 1977)
- Lao Tsu, *Tao Te Ching* [tr. Gia Fu Feng and Jane English] (Wildwood House, 1973)

FRAMEWORK – MODELS

Summary

Models are often the most visible part of architecture work. Each model-type represents a different way to describe a specific business context, in terms of architectural entities and relationships between those entities. At the whole-of-enterprise scope, there are significant issues with access-control, model versioning and model dynamics that need to be addressed.

Details

Models – an overview

To many people, models *are* architecture, though for those of us who do the work in architecture they're just one of many possible outcomes of what we do. There's no doubt, though, that those impressive-looking diagrams that we can churn out from a good EA toolset do help, not just in clarifying our thinking, but also our credibility. Models *matter*.

> My mother was a family-doctor back in the days when there weren't that many women in 'the trade'. She always kept a stethoscope close to hand, even though she used it only occasionally – because its presence assured her patients that she was a *real* doctor...
>
> Much the same for enterprise-architects, too. All those pretty pictures with their arrays of arcane symbols might not mean that much in practice, if we're honest about it, but in our clients' eyes they're part of the proof that we know what we're doing. Possibly...
>
> Just don't mistake them for the real thing, though: a model is a map, but the map is not the territory. The real architecture is often invisible, about ways of thinking, ways of relating within an enterprise: a model is an *aid* in that process, not the thing itself. Models matter: we just need to be clear how and why and for what purposes they matter – and not get lost in making models for models' sake.

A model is a description, a prescription and a prediction about the nature and characteristics of a 'world'. The model describes what is in that world and what is not, what we expect to happen there, how we expect it to be and to behave. In the case of enterprise architecture, that 'world' is some aspect of the enterprise – *any* aspect, from the broadest high-level strategy to the minutiae of low-level technical detail.

Models are often presented in the form of visual diagrams, but that doesn't always need to be the case; and conversely, not all diagrams are models. The *real* model is the set of descriptions and relationships that underlie the diagram; and the whole point of the model itself is that it's something that is of practical *use*, in helping to make sense of complexity, and in guiding decisions and responses to change.

Each model describes the 'world' from a specific view and view-point. No one model describes *everything* – so we'll need multiple models, and multiple *types* of models, to make sense of a complete context. A model will describe a set of entities and the relation-ships between them – content, context and connections. Each model will also need its own descriptive metadata, to place it within a specific business context; and most models will need to be managed under some form of version-control, to keep track of dynamic changes over time.

Model views and viewpoints

As with the architecture itself, every model needs to exist for a practical purpose. To have any value to the business, it needs to have a business reason. And for each model, we also need to be clear about how it supports the *overall* business purpose – and whose interests it serves within that business purpose.

Most of this would be addressed in the earlier stages of the archi-tecture cycle – see 'Phase A – establish iteration scope' (p.122) and 'Phase B – assess current context' (p.128) in *Methodology – assessment*. But this is also where we need to clarify the differences between two similar-seeming terms: views, and viewpoints.

A *view* is a single view or summary into some aspect of the overall business 'world', and provides a common language – or at least a common means – to describe that view of the 'world'. A view can be expressed as a model, or just a simpler descriptive diagram; in effect, a *model-type* is almost synonymous with 'view', though often it'd be more that a cluster of closely-related models and diagrams would provide that view.

A *viewpoint* is the perspective, onto the whole, of a single stake-holder or defined group of stakeholders. It's a *focus*, an area of interest. So we define a viewpoint not in terms of model-types as such, but in terms of those stakeholders and their interests and concerns. To cover the whole of the enterprise, we will need to define a very broad set of viewpoints.

The definition of a viewpoint, in turn, implies the requirements for a set of related views. But the point here is that there's a many-to-many relationship between them: each viewpoint may require many different views, some of which are useful only to that viewpoint; but some views will be relevant to many different stakeholders, and hence would be associated with many viewpoints. Viewpoints *connect* through their shared views, which represent their shared concerns – a key point in itself as we start to look to architecture to help integration across the enterprise.

> The TOGAF specification includes a useful section on views and viewpoints. As usual, though, it's too incomplete and too IT-centric to be all that much help at the whole-of-enterprise level: a good starting-point, but ultimately a bit frustrating. Oh well.
>
> There's a list of viewpoints with a rather broader reach at the Agile Enterprise Architecture website; and some of the military-oriented frameworks such as DODAF and MODAF can give valuable hints, too, because they *do* know about a world beyond the bounds of IT.
>
> But the simplest way to grasp this is to recognise that every stakeholder has their own perspective on the whole – in other words, their own specific viewpoint. That viewpoint is unique, but the views it will use are not. So which views – or model-types – do the users of that viewpoint need in order to make sense of their part of the enterprise? What views do they need to share with others, and how and when and where and why? If you start from there, the distinctions between views and viewpoints will begin to make sense.

To illustrate the difference between view and viewpoint, the TOGAF specification uses an aircraft example:

- the *pilot*'s focus (or viewpoint) is on management of the aircraft;
- the *air-traffic controller*'s focus is on the management of airspace;
- their interests (and views) coincide on the management of that specific aircraft in the airspace.

It's a good example, though it doesn't really cover the *dynamics* of views and viewpoints. To illustrate that, it's useful to extend that example a bit further, with three distinct traffic-control roles:

- the *airspace controller* manages many aircraft in the space between airports, including general-aviation light aircraft, gliders and balloons – which might not have radio communication with traffic-control – and also coordinating with military traffic-control;

- the *airport controller* manages a single stream of aircraft in the air, during the period when they take off and come in to land at that specific airport;
- the *ground controller* manages aircraft once they're on the ground, along with all the other vehicles of various shapes and sizes moving around on 'airside' at the airport.

These are distinct realms of interest – distinct viewpoints – with distinct handovers between them. To the pilot, these handovers should be seamless: from that viewpoint, it should all seem to be one 'air traffic control'. We'll see the same partitioning between aviation meteorologists: their common interest is weather, but at different scales, from international, national, regional and airport-specific. Again, the pilot would want to know about each of these, for essential information about tail-winds, or clear-air turbulence, or wind-shear on approach; but unlike air-traffic controllers, the meteorologists would have little interest in individual aircraft, and probably no direct communication with them at all.

From the viewpoint of the passengers, of course, all these technical details would be unimportant: to them, the flight would be an amorphous 'black box' between departure and arrival. *They* just want to get on with the journey – an overall 'business process' in which the airport and aircraft are merely intermediate stages.

Each of the views from these viewpoints will have different levels of abstraction, different timescales, and so on, and the content will vary over time even though the model-types may remain much the same. Viewpoints are fairly static; the views they use are less so; and the content of individual models can be very dynamic indeed – as in an air-traffic controller's real-time display. Each to their own: but we do need to be clear at all times as to which is which.

Model entities and relationships

The viewpoint determines who the model is for; the view determines what should be in (and not in) the model. And the model-type determines how the information should be structured within the model. In essence, a model is made up of three types of items, of which only the first are actually required:

- **entities**, the *nouns* or 'things' of the model – the primitives and composites from the framework and repository
- **relationships**, the *verbs* or actions of the model
- **attributes**, the *adjectives* or qualities of the things and relationships in the model

(There's also a fourth type of information, namely metadata, but we'll come back to that in the next section.)

> You'll notice that nothing's been said about how these items are displayed on the screen, the page or whatever. That's deliberate: in fact it's really, *really* important to keep presentation separate from content. A model-standard may require a particular layout and so on, but it's essential not to lock ourselves into that layout alone if we're going to be able to re-use the same content elsewhere.
>
> As for why, here's a real example from our work with a large logistics organisation. We were presenting a fairly complex issue at board-level about the impact of a set of change-projects on their overall logistics network. First time round we made the fatal mistake of presenting the process-flows as BPMN (Business Process Modelling Notation) diagrams. All clean, simple, nicely abstract; we understood those diagrams perfectly. But the board didn't: the sarcastic comment of "what the heck is *that* supposed to mean?" was better than the blank stares we got from everyone else. Yup, we ran away from that meeting as fast as we could... though they did give us a chance to try again.
>
> So we rebuilt the diagrams, replacing all those bland BPMN boxes with pictures of conveyor-belts, sorting-machines, fork-lifts, pallets, trucks and so on. Underneath, it was exactly the same model, the same semantics and suchlike, the same formal rigour. But this time it *did* make sense to the board – they could *see* what it all meant, where the previous abstractions had in effect *hidden* the meaning from them. We got our go-ahead all right: presentation *matters*.
>
> The catch was that we couldn't do it within our main EA toolset: it insisted that BPMN was the only permissible presentation for a process model. Instead, we had to export the model and do a horrible hack-job in Visio to make it all work – and then couldn't re-import any process-changes because we'd changed the graphics. Nightmare...
>
> Moral of this story? Keep content as separate as possible from presentation, every step of the way – because every time you merge them, you're creating pain for yourself somewhere down the line.

A model describes behaviours in relation to its entities. That's why a diagram is not always a model: it'd be descriptive, in a way, but unless it's showing some kind of relationship, or prescription, it's not really a model.

There's also a matter of scope and abstraction, which is where there's a crosslink to the layering of the framework – see *Framework – layers*, p.59. The simplest possible model, right up at row-0 or row-1, the 'Scope' layer, is a straightforward list: it's a model because it prescribes both what is and, implicitly, what is not included in that context. At row-2, the 'Business' layer, we add explicit relationships between entities; and at row-3, the 'Logical' layer, we add sufficient attributes – which themselves are often also relationships to other entities or lists – to be able to do more descriptive designs.

There are hundreds – more like thousands – of different model-types, so there's no point in even trying to list them here. There are the obvious common ones, of course, such as org-charts and data-models and parts-breakdown schemas; but each industry and professional discipline will have model upon model of their own, and most of us in real-world enterprise-architecture practice will find ourselves tweaking some of those, or designing something from scratch, in order to support some special modelling need.

Which is why it seems amazing that some EA toolset vendors still present a single model-type for each Zachman cell, and provide no means to do anything more than that. Which is useless, frankly: we *must* be able to build our own model-types, and with the appropriate level of modelling rigour for each, too. Yet another item to add to that toolset-requirements checklist...

Most model-types will create links horizontally across a single framework row: a process-model is the obvious example, linking capabilities and roles, events, services, assets and decisions. Those model-types that build links between layers – such as logical-to-physical data-transforms, or organisation-designs – will demand a kind of conceptual shift at each change of layer, so for sanity's sake they're usually restricted to a single framework column.

We can go wider than that if necessary, but there's no way that we could build a single 'universal model', one that covers *everything*, in every layer, column and segment: it's too big, too complex, and even trying to do so would be a certain recipe for instant insanity. Hence the value of views and viewpoints; but hence also the need to be able to hold as many of them in mind as we can, switching between them to build and maintain a better sense of the whole.

The model-type defines the 'legal' or permitted types of relationships between entities in the model. As with 'bindedness' of the use of entities in reference frameworks – see 'Composites and 'completeness'' in *Framework – composites*, p.85 – it's useful to apply a Cynefin or MoSCoW approach to the bindedness of relationships in models: some will be mandatory, some recommended, others merely optional. For example, in a BPMN model, every process *must* have a starting-event, *should* specify the assets ('data-objects') used in each process, *could* include descriptive comments about the process, and (like 'can *wait*') *might* include comments about past or future versions of the process.

Once again many of the existing EA toolsets can be more of a hindrance than a help in this, because the way they manage entity-relationships in models is all the wrong way round.

93

Perhaps it's because it's the easiest way to implement a metamodel: I don't know. But the usual way it's done in the toolsets is that entities are designed first – which is fair enough. There's then a list of 'legal' relationships defined for each of those entities (though some toolsets don't allow us to design our own, forcing us to stick with their predefined sets instead). Model-types come along later, almost as an afterthought, specifying the entity-types that are allowed in the model, and then picking a relationship from what is often a huge catalogue of possibles. Many of these are either inappropriate or irrelevant to the model-type, and often leading to inappropriate or irrelevant entities. Enforcing modelling-rigour becomes a lot harder this way round, too.

Instead, to make it work, we need a shift in perspective: *the relationship and its bindedness are attributes of the model-type, not the entity.* That list of 'legal' relationships then inherently implies the list of entities that can be included in the model. Beneath that, in effect ,there's just one generic relationship, a kind of always-optional '‹is related to›' which we can link from any entity to any other, and which we can label in any way we like – but it's not binding in any way, it's just a perceived link of some kind. Any other relationship, with any tighter bindedness, is part of a model-type – which also immediately specifies the validations we need for modelling-rigour. So we don't have a huge catalogue of possible relationships attached to each entity-type: instead, we have a list of *model-types* in which we can use that entity.

And because there's that generic '‹is related to›' relationship available between every entity, we can always build a free-form model – a new 'view' – linking anything to anything else. Then as we gain a sense of what does and doesn't need to be enforced in that view, we can start to apply levels of bindedness to those relationships, perhaps with their own attributes, too – which means we've now defined a new enforceable model-type. This gives us the flexibility we need for architecture modelling – which we don't get from the back-to-front way the existing toolsets give us.

Something to think about, anyway…

Every relationship has its own attributes, such as its unique ID, name, description, direction (unidirectional, bidirectional or neutral) and bindedness. And in addition to the explicit relationships we'll see on the page or screen, model-types may also include a variety of *implicit* relationships, such as:

- *containment* – for example, process-step within a BPMN swimlane, or a function contained within a higher-scope function in a layered business-function model
- *include-by-reference* – for example, lookup for a predefined set of attribute values
- layering of composites – relationships between a composite and its component composites and primitives

These implicit relationships may also need their own attributes, such as 'soft' bindedness where a process-step could be done by more than one capability or role – in other words, preferred role in a shared swimlane. Unfortunately, few of the existing EA toolsets will manage this consistently, if at all; but we do need to be aware of the need for it, and why.

Model metadata, versioning and dynamics

Models and model-types are 'entities' in their own right – and should be treated as such in the repository – so they too require their own supporting metadata.

Of these, probably the most important are version-identifiers and the like. Some of the most difficult problems in modelling revolve around keeping track of model-versions: the model, and everything in it, has its own lifecycle, and there is no stable 'future state'. Over time, any or all of the entities, relationships and attributes referenced in a model may change; so even if the model itself appears to stay the same, we need to know which versions of each of these content-items applies to what at any given moment, in any given project or suchlike.

So we *need* a proper system of version-identifiers, for *everything* in every model. Without them, trying to keep track of what applies when and where – and dealing with the consequences of failing to do so – will soon become a nightmare. Versioning *matters*.

> And yes, this is yet another area where the existing EA toolsets let us down: many seem to assume that once a model has been created, neither it nor its content will ever change. So far I've only seen one toolset that made a serious attempt to tackle the issues properly – but unfortunately it was almost the only part of toolset-usability they *did* get right...
>
> In any other toolset, at present, you'll have to invent some kind of work-around to give you the versioning you'll need. The usual way to do this is via naming-conventions with embedded version-identifiers: it's ugly and long-winded, but it works. If you do this, define it as part of your Architecture Standards – and make sure everyone sticks to it religiously, because if you let anyone be lax about it, it'll cause chaos further down the track.
>
> Remember, too, to remind people that any such workaround *is* only a short-term kludge, and should itself be treated like any other architecture 'dispensation' – see summary in *Basics – the architecture process*, p.16 – to be reviewed regularly, and replaced by a proper solution as soon as possible.

This is especially complicated in modelling for the multi-partner enterprise, such as in consortia, or the whole of a supply-chain from supplier's supplier to customer's customer. In most cases we can't enforce anything beyond the boundaries of our own organisation; but we need to be able to share models, entity-definitions, entity-relationships and the like across the whole enterprise; and we need to be able to keep track of versions across that whole context, too.

But other than a few specifications that in practice are only for low-level software architecture, there are as yet no standards for information interchange here; and none that seem to handle version-metadata and the like. So it's likely that for some years at least we'll be on our own in this, and have to make do with whatever we can find that seems to work. The key point, though, is that we need to acknowledge that some kind of standards for this interchange *are* essential, and include specifications for them in the shared Architecture Standards we develop with our enterprise partners.

Application

- What models do you create in your architecture? From what model-types?
- In what ways and for what purposes do you use each model-type?
- What standards and standard model-specifications do you use in your models? What is the business value of using those particular standards, and not others?
- With whom do you share your models? Why, and for what purposes? Who are the users of those models, both within your organisation, and outside of it in the broader enterprise?
- How do you handle versioning and other model-dynamics? By what means do you control access to models? – to define and manage 'need to know, need to use'?

Resources

- Zachman framework: see www.zifa.org
- TOGAF on views and viewpoints: see www.opengroup.org/architecture/togaf8-doc/arch/toc.html (chapter 'Developing Architecture Views')
- Example views at Agile Enterprise Architecture: see agileea.wikidot.com/views

FRAMEWORK – INTEGRATION

Summary

At root, the framework needs to make it possible to describe, visualise and model every aspect of the enterprise – whatever form the enterprise may take, and whatever way it may change. This demands a great deal of flexibility, not just in the framework, but in the way we perceive the enterprise and the architecture process.

Details

Integration – an overview

The architecture framework is about more than models and other 'pretty pictures': its real purpose is as a means to describe the way everything in the enterprise connects with everything else. In other words, about integration of the enterprise *as* a whole.

For the framework, there are three key themes in this integration:

- key descriptive *metaphors* for the enterprise
- *interdependency* across the enterprise
- shared *language* to describe the enterprise

The metaphors we use about the enterprise are critical, because they act as filters on how we perceive it, and thence on what we can and cannot do within it. As described earlier – see 'A matter of metaphor' in *Purpose – an overview*, p.22 – probably the key comparison is between the metaphors of 'enterprise as machine' and 'enterprise as living organism': the former is usable for low-level integration, but at the whole-of-enterprise scope, the latter is far more effective. Whichever we choose, though, the framework needs to be structured to support and reinforce that metaphor.

The framework needs to describe how everything fits together: hence a necessary emphasis on interdependence between different functions, services, business-rules, policies, business-units and so on – all of the items that we describe in models as relationships between entities. There are many ways to describe these myriad interdependencies, but perhaps the simplest is that of the 'service-oriented enterprise' – describing everything in the enterprise as a 'service' of some kind. Service-orientation is well-understood as an IT-architecture concept, but less well known at the whole-of-enterprise level, so it's worthwhile taking some time to explore how the framework can best support it.

And description always depends on a common 'language' of some kind, a shared grammar and syntax – verbal, visual or whatever – from which meaning can be derived and communication made possible. The complication here is that each business culture, each 'silo' sub-culture and professional discipline has its own language, its own peculiar terminology and meanings; and somehow, at the whole-of-enterprise level, we have to link all those 'languages' together. But when 'the enterprise' may be any subset *or superset* of the organisation, this isn't easy... especially when the effective boundaries of 'the enterprise' may be changing dynamically from day to day. So we need to explore, too, how the framework can help in resolving some of these complications.

Integration – organisation as organism

Almost all existing 'enterprise architecture' frameworks imply a metaphor of 'engineering the enterprise'. The metaphor is explicit in most of Zachman's work, for example. But whilst it works well enough at the low-level implementation layers, it's *not* good at the whole-of-enterprise level, because it excludes almost every idea of purpose, and most of the issues around people *as* people.

Instead, as we saw earlier, a more viable metaphor is that of 'the living organisation'. This leads us to focus more on 'nurturing' the enterprise rather than attempts at 'engineering'. The conventional IT-centric reference-frameworks are full of the 'things' we would expect to 'engineer' – fixed standards for applications, servers, routers, data-schemas and the like – and those would still apply at the implementation-layer parts of any framework for the 'living organisation'. But to those elements we would add the items we would also expect to see in a living organisation – particularly *people*, and *purpose*.

Hence, as described earlier, the need for that extra dimension of 'segments' for the Zachman-type framework for primitives – see *Framework – primitives*, p.63 – and also the additional 'Universals' layer – see *Framework – layers*, p.59. The former provides the depth that we need; the latter a permanent anchor for the framework, as a stable point around which everything else can change.

> Perhaps an alternative to 'anchor' would be 'guiding star', but either way the point is that it's something stable in an unstable world. To be

honest, we don't need it all that much when our world *is* stable – the metaphoric equivalent of pootling back and forth along the same old coastal commute. In those uncomplicated, almost carefree conditions, we can sit back and concentrate on efficiency and the like, because there's not much else to worry about. But when the weather turns from placid calm to full-blown tempest, or we suddenly find ourselves in uncharted waters... *that's* when we need a stable reference-point, and an urgent emphasis on overall effectiveness rather than only on efficiency and 'engineering'. *That's* when we need all the human factors – and every other extra edge we can find – to be properly represented in our architecture framework.

When the world is stable, everything seems merely *mechanical*: so it's easy to see how a simplistic idea like 'engineering the enterprise' can take hold. But when a perfect storm hits – such as, at the time I write this, the worst failure of the financial system for almost a hundred years – *that's* when the enterprise comes alive: because if it doesn't, we're dead. Metaphorically speaking, anyway.

In the classic 'engineering'-style reference-frameworks, the main emphasis is on the items listed in the framework – all the boxes and components and so on. But in the living-enterprise metaphor we need to concern ourselves as much, if not more, with the links *between* those entities – because those are what connect everything together into that unified whole.

Some of those connections are about computer-based information-sharing, as in the usual IT-centric views of enterprise architecture. But we need to be just as much concerned with the non-IT-based information, through social-networks and other interchanges of personal or 'tacit' knowledge. We need to map not only the skills and capabilities available to us in the enterprise – some of them embedded in IT-systems, or in other machines – but also the means by which these capabilities are developed, expanded, maintained, transferred from one person to another. And we also need to track how the enterprise adapts itself to changing circumstances, and applies its processes of continuing improvement in that changing world.

Once we have these items in the framework – or at least places where we know they would fit – we're prepared for the 'perfect storm'. Agility, flexibility, versatility, adaptability, resilience: these are qualities we *need* in the enterprise – so we must ensure that the framework we create for the 'living enterprise' will support them.

Integration – the service-oriented enterprise

To make sense of all that complexity, we need some kind of overview that remains consistent at every level: and for that purpose, one of the most valuable concepts is that of the 'service-oriented enterprise' – extending the IT-based concept of 'service-oriented architecture' (SOA), all the way up to a whole-of-enterprise scope.

One framework I've found useful for this is Stafford Beer's proven Viable System Model (VSM), as it provides an explicit template of the relationships needed for completeness of mutual support between services. It also in effect describes the information-paths required for key performance-indicators, critical success-factors and the like that are needed to monitor service performance.

It's perhaps best to step back a bit to explain this. In a service-oriented view of the enterprise, every business process is a net-work of transactions between services: and *everything* is a service. In abstract terms, each service consists of two interdependent layers: service-delivery, which does the deliverable work of the service; and service-management sub-systems to monitor and guide that service-delivery. We could call these respectively the 'brawn' and the 'brain' of the service: but we need to remember that they always exist as an interlinked pair.

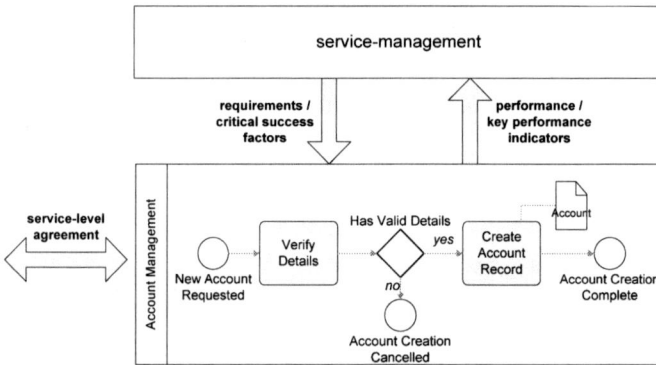

A simple example of a business function as a service

IT-based SOA is concerned mostly with the low-level choreo-graphy of services and their underlying mechanisms, so its usual emphasis is on 'brawn to brawn' connections – the service trans-actions through mechanisms such as an enterprise service bus, and, in a more mature implementation, conditions and metrics to monitor the service-level agreements (SLAs) and operational level agreements (OLAs) with other services. In terms of time, this all happens in the 'now'. But performance-metrics such as key per-formance indicators (KPIs) and critical success factors (CSFs) are almost invisible at this level, and monitoring in general often seems to be tackled only as an afterthought.

Yet in a true service-oriented architecture we need to know as much about the service's 'brain' as its 'brawn'. We need to keep track of what's going on, through all the KPIs and CSFs and so on – which also include the KPIs, CSFs and SLAs that link *between* the layers. We also need a broader sense of time than just the 'now': we need to picture what's happened in the past, and prepare and plan for the future. This information needs to pass up and down the layers through a web of other inter-linked services. Even in IT service-management, many of these 'brain' services can be done only by people, not machines: so to make this work, we *must* expand our view of SOA beyond the 'IT-only' box.

The 'brawn + brain' pairs don't exist in isolation: it's more useful to think of them as stacked in layers, services 'enclosed' within more abstract business-services and functions. Working upward from real-time service-delivery, each 'brain + brawn' pair becomes the 'brawn' of the next level up. Results for KPIs and suchlike migrate upward for a business view of service-delivery; and we 'drill down' to see the detail.

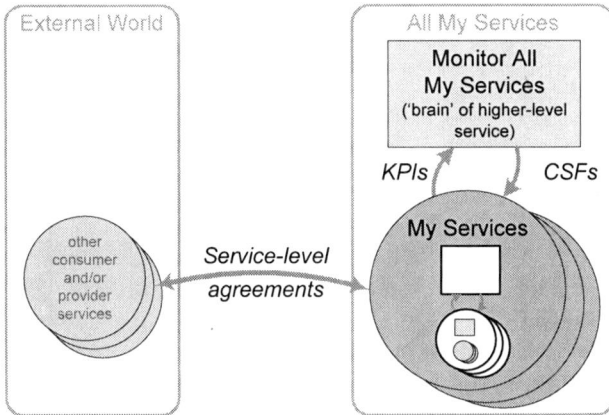

Hierarchy of services, each with their own performance-measures

This layering maps closely to the layering of the framework. At the row-0 level, the entire enterprise can be viewed as a single service, with the principles, values and so on in that row providing the ultimate anchors for the trails of KPIs and CSFs.

We can also see this layering in the way that root-level transaction-data is transformed into business-information, and then knowledge, as it moves upward, and links across the columns of the framework; we just hope that somewhere it does also become wisdom!

This pattern of *recursion*, as each 'brawn + brain' pair becomes a 'brawn' for the next layer up, is a core principle of the Viable System Model. The VSM focuses on management-support – on guiding-principles and the future view as well as day-to-day management. In abstract terms, each service has the same set of sub-systems for specific tasks – though note that choreography (system-2) and quality-audit (system-3*) exist partly outside of the main management hierarchy.

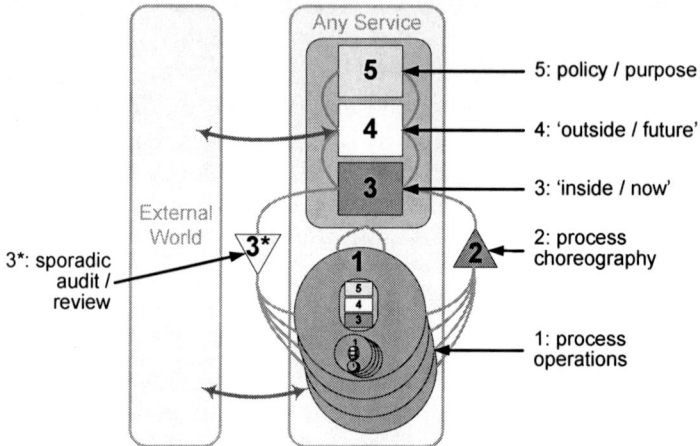

Specialised sub-systems with each service in Viable System Model

For the overall enterprise to be 'viable' – especially in the longer term – all these sub-systems need to exist in *every* layer and *every* service in the enterprise. In the machine-metaphor, the 'brain' is entirely separate from 'brawn', and exists in only one place – the management. But in the Viable System Model, as a description of the 'living enterprise' metaphor, the 'brain' is distributed through-out the entire enterprise, applying context-specific knowledge and skill at the point closest to the action. This leads to greater agility and innovation, and faster response to incidents and to change.

For service-management we'll also need to know more about the interactions *between* 'systems'. This extends the VSM to a 'viable *services* model', giving us a means to categorise services in a way which maps well to the living-enterprise metaphor:

- *delivery-services* to external service-consumers: 'muscular system' (also 'digestive system' etc as service-delivery for internal systems and services)
- *information-services* and point-to-point information-flows: 'nervous system'

- *infrastructure-services* such as building-management, energy-distribution, logistics, waste-management etc: 'skeletal system', 'vascular system' etc
- *pervasive-services* for distributed, pervasive actions and information-flows such as security, quality management, knowledge management, business-ethics, health safety and environment: 'endocrine system'

In effect, this extended viable services model provides a map of the interfaces needed for the service-oriented enterprise: each interdependency between services also implies a need for some kind of interface between them. We can also use this, mapped against our architecture framework, to model 'service complete-ness': for the enterprise as a whole to be viable, links to all the standard VSM 'systems' must be identifiable for every service; and, for optimum service-performance, direct or indirect links to all other needed services should be identifiable – particularly the hormone-like 'pervasive services' which ultimately anchor everything back to the row-0 principles, policies and vision.

This mapping is also relevant from an IT-architecture perspective. Each link identifies an interdependence between services: so each also implies a need for information-system support in some form. An information-link would not always be computer-based – it might be the information content of a review-meeting, perhaps, or just an everyday conversation – but an information exchange of some kind still needs to take place in every case.

Integration – boundary effects

As with governance, many of the most difficult problems for the framework occur at the edges – particularly where 'the enterprise' has different boundaries than those of the organisation, because we run into inevitable issues of governance and jurisdiction. One of the most common sources for such problems revolves around *definition*, around what terms to use, and what they each mean – because not only does every organisation have its own distinctive terminology, but every silo, every discipline, even every work-team. If we're not careful about this, we can end up with absolute Babel… and huge risks for the enterprise architecture.

The standard approach to a solution is to demand a single fixed 'official definition' for every possible term. But whilst we can sort-of make it work within a sub-domain of a single small business unit, it falls apart rapidly as we expand the scope. We can impose a specific subset of language for a specific need, but that's about it.

> A professional institute down the road from here teaches 'Aviation English' – the international standard language for air-traffic control. Talking with an instructor there, she emphasises that it's not English as such, but a 'trade language' that uses a small subset of an English-like grammar and vocabulary for its own specific needs.
>
> It is a distinct language in its own right, and prior knowledge of English can be more of a hindrance than a help – in fact native English-speakers are some of the worst culprits in misusing it. It's true that a clipped, formal "Kilo Alpha, wind bearing one seven zero degrees gusting up to four zero knots across Runway Zero Niner Left" doesn't have quite the same poetic ring as a Southern drawl of "Y'all is gonna git crawsswindid t'hill on th' frueewhye", but at least it's possible for 'foreigners' to understand it!

In Cynefin terms, relying on fixed dictionary-definitions is like trying to use a rule-based approach in the complex domain: we might perhaps delude ourselves that we can make it work, but it's inevitably asking for trouble. Instead, as Cynefin suggests, we have to work *with* the complexity: which means first accepting that there's no such thing as '*the* definition'.

So whilst a standard glossary is an essential item to underpin our framework, we need to back it up with a sophisticated thesaurus and cross-reference – see 'Glossary and Thesaurus' in *Completion – architecture artefacts*, p.182. Ideally, this needs to extend into the metamodel and item definitions in the architecture toolset – but few if any of the current crop of toolsets can support this as yet.

> If we can't embed it in the toolset, we can at least embed it in the everyday activities of the enterprise. One of our clients constructed an excellent 'jargon buster' tool with a lookup field in the base-template of their intranet, so that it was available from every page. It included definitions, synonyms, antonyms, 'sounds-like' matching and so on, all linked to brief summaries of practical applications. It was built as a moderated wiki, such that anyone could post definitions and updates, but it was monitored and maintained overall by the organisation's knowledge-management team.
>
> Cheap, simple, very effective, very successful in every sense – including reducing cost and risk. Strongly recommended.

The same applies to every other aspect of the framework: we need some consistent means to exchange information, but in a context where there are almost no usable standards. So to a significant extent you're on your own at present: you'll need to negotiate a suitable 'standard' with your enterprise partners, and share as best you can. But the first stage, perhaps, is to acknowledge that it *is* a real issue that you'll have to face in any true enterprise architecture – and expand outward from there.

Application

- How do you use your existing architecture frameworks to tie the enterprise together? What would you need to amend or add, to improve this integration?

- Do your existing frameworks view the enterprise only as some kind of machine, as an arbitrary collection of components without any inherent purpose? If so, what would you need to amend or add so as to support the 'living enterprise' metaphor?

- Does your framework already support a 'service-oriented architecture'? If so, is it only for low-level IT, or can it extend across the whole enterprise?

- Do you have an enterprise glossary and thesaurus? If so, to what extent is it integrated with your enterprise architecture? What could you do to enhance that integration?

- What are the boundary-issues for your existing architecture? How does your architecture manage the difference between 'organisation' and 'enterprise' – especially when the bounds of the enterprise extend beyond the borders of the organisation? What issues arise for management of your frameworks in such circumstances?

Resources

Viable System Model: see en.wikipedia.org/wiki/Viable_System_Model

Viable System Model: Stafford Beer, *Brain of the Firm* (Allen Lane: The Penguin Press, 1972)

Integration architecture: Tom Graves, *Real Enterprise Architecture: beyond IT to the whole enterprise* (Tetradian, 2008)

Human factors in enterprise: Tom Graves, *Power and Response-ability: the human side of systems* (Tetradian, 2008)

METHODOLOGY – AN OVERVIEW

Summary

A formal methodology specifies the structure and sequence – the how, where and when – for architecture activities. To maintain familiarity for IT-architects, the methodology described here is adapted from the Architecture Design Method (ADM) of the Open Group framework (TOGAF), expanded to suit the broader scope and complexity of whole-of-enterprise architecture.

Details

Methodology and governance

Purpose identifies the 'why' of the architecture-cycle, governance circumscribes the 'who', and the framework describes much of the 'what', the means to derive meaning from what is discovered. Next we need methodology, to specify the 'how', 'when' and 'where' – the structure and sequence for the activities, the actual *process* of architecture.

The methodology is where we start to put all the ideas into practice. Up till now it's all been somewhat theoretical, abstract; but here we need to *do* something – and something that has practical *use*.

There are two radically different approaches we can take to this. In the classic 'hands-on' approach – which we'll explore in this and the next few chapters – architecture drives design: there'll be a strong emphasis on development of 'blueprints', 'roadmaps for change' and standard reference-models, and an insistence on compliance to those models. This style is typical, and usually appropriate, in large organisations and in the earlier stages or architecture development. The catch is that unless we're careful, it can become cumbersome and bureaucratic, ensuring compliance at the cost of agility. To resolve this, the other approach, which we'll explore later in *Methodology – hands-off architecture* (see p.161) goes to the opposite extreme, allowing design and consistency to emerge from the natural complexity of everyday architectural choices.

Whichever way we do it, we need strong links to governance, to ensure that what we do *is* of practical use to the enterprise. The governance processes are there to ensure that architecture does indeed begin with a business purpose; those processes ensure appropriate actions by the appropriate people at each stage in creating and implementing the architecture.

Methodology implements governance; governance maintains accountability in the methodology

So whilst we might describe the activities in terms of a methodology, we need to embed governance *within* that methodology. The standard TOGAF ADM methodology does this for IT architecture, for example, in calling for stakeholder reviews at various points in the ADM cycle.

But here we hit a problem of scale. The classic 'big bang' approach to enterprise architecture requires us to develop 'as-is' and 'to-be' architecture descriptions for the entire scope – which could literally take years, just for the IT-architecture alone, and most probably be well out of date long before the process is completed. But for anything smaller, TOGAF's requirement for *dozens* of stakeholder-reviews is clearly going to be overkill: if we call a stakeholder-review every week, it won't be long before no-one bothers to turn up – which in effect means no governance. So we need an approach to governance that will give us the right balance for architecture-cycles at every scale, from quick assessment-projects to mid-size change-programmes and portfolio management, up to full-scale business transformation.

The same applies to the methodology itself: it too needs to be usable *and consistent* at every scale. We need something that is scalable, yet in essence uses the same steps and sequence, whether the business purpose requires activities that will take half a day or half a year. The classic IT-architecture methodologies, such as FEAF and TOGAF, only describe the full-scale 'big-bang', in a strict 'Waterfall' style: it's clear we'll to rethink this approach if we're going to have a methodology that we *can* use at every scale.

It must be dozens of times now that would-be clients have asked us to develop an architecture "in accordance with the Zachman methodology". They often get quite upset when we explain that we can't do so, for the simple reason that it doesn't exist. Zachman himself has been promising for years to provide one, but to date he

> still hasn't published anything: the nearest that's available is in his architecture seminars.
>
> But in the absence of an explicit methodology, people often invent something, *anything*, that seems to fit the Zachman framework. So given Zachman's exhortation that ultimately we need to assess everything in "excruciating detail", the putative architects plod their way through every cell of the original framework, twice – once for 'as-is', and once for 'to-be' – modelling Zachman's root-composites as if they're primitives, and ignoring the real usable composites. Which is not only insanely time-consuming, but also, as we've seen, too misleading and incomplete even for IT-architecture, let alone true whole-of-enterprise architecture. Worse, there's no means to link in any kind of systematic governance at all – a guaranteed recipe for problems. *Not* recommended...

Of the current crop of methodologies, TOGAF version 8.1 'Enterprise Edition' is probably our best choice. The original ADM is perhaps more of a hindrance than a help for whole-of-enterprise architecture, because it's set up only for 'big-bang' development, and so rigidly IT-centric that *everything* not-IT is dismissed as 'Business Architecture'. But we can make it usable for any scale and scope of architecture-work by tweaking the definitions and the sequence of some of the activities in some of the ADM's Phases – particularly in Phases A-D – and adding more systematic links to governance.

The architecture cycle

The architecture cycle in the TOGAF ADM in effect follows the same project-lifecycle as we're using here – Purpose, People, Preparation, Process and Performance. This is perhaps not obvious because there are *two* interleaving cycles: one for the assessment phases – the architecture proper – and one for solution-designs arising from the assessments. At this level, the main difference between the ADM and what we're doing here is that we're not restricted to constructing an IT-architecture: we can use the same methodology and Phase sequence for architecture at *any* scale, and for any framework scope.

The modified TOGAF ADM cycle described here and in the next few chapters also maps well with PRINCE2 and similar programme or project management methodologies and governance. For example, unlike the original ADM, we now have just one explicit stakeholder-review at the end of each of the Phases A to D. The key governance documents or 'products' also mark the boundaries between the architecture-cycle Phases.

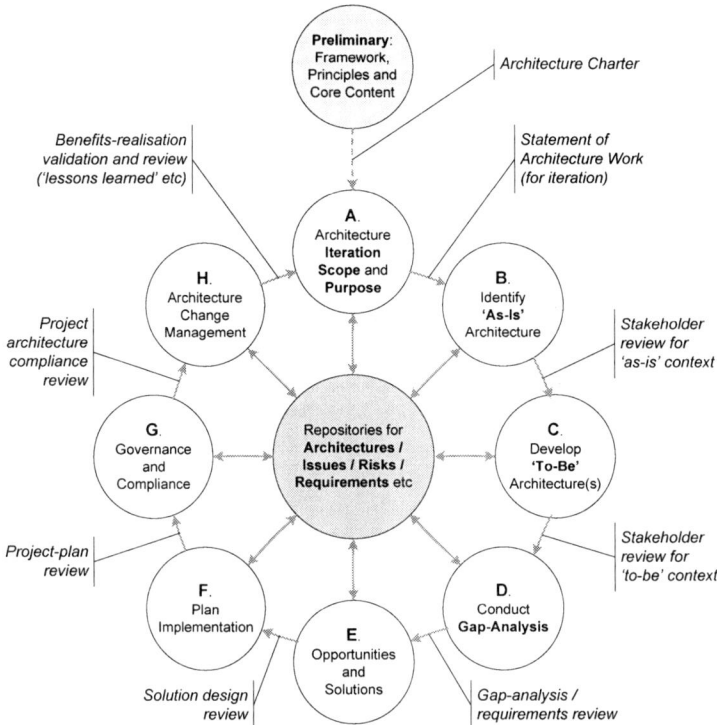

Governance-artefacts define architecture-cycle's phase-boundaries

Before we can do any architecture development, we need to set up the architecture capability itself. To do this, we 'boot' the architecture via a high-level version of the *same* architecture-cycle. In TOGAF, this is described as the 'Preliminary Phase'.

- **Phase P**: *Preliminaries* – establish (or review) the architecture capability, the purpose, governance, framework, methodology and completion, and define a big-picture view of what the overall aims to achieve for the entire enterprise

During the preliminary phase we define the key documents such as the Architecture Charter, and also set up the repositories and registers that are at the core of the architecture cycle: requirements, issues and risks, glossary and thesaurus, architecture-dispensations, governance-records and the architecture repository itself.

Once this is done, and the governance and the like formally approved, we're now ready to fill in the detail of the architecture and apply it in practice. A key point here is that unlike the assumptions in IT-centric architectures such as FEAF or TOGAF, we *know* that what we're dealing with at a whole-of-enterprise level is too large to tackle in one go. So we start from the clear knowledge that we're going to do this iteratively, with each step constrained within the relatively narrow scope of a single business issue or change-project. This approach works because we're using a framework that has a true enterprise-wide coverage. It also makes better business sense, because we gain some immediate return from the architecture work, and the value increases steadily as each project leverages the knowledge and lessons learned from previous architecture cycles.

In the TOGAF specification, the scope and purpose are pre-defined: it's always IT-centric architecture, with a strong emphasis on detail-level technology. But here we may be dealing with *any* scope, *any* business-issue. So if you're familiar with TOGAF, note that the first four Phases here each have a subtly different emphasis from what you may be used to:

- **Phase A**: *Establish iteration scope* – identify the core business-issue(s) to be addressed, and scope (in terms of framework layers, columns and segments) to be covered in the analysis
- **Phase B**: *Assess current context* – establish the current architectural description for the scope and business-issue identified in Phase A
- **Phase C**: *Assess future context* – establish the required future-architecture for the scope and business-issue identified in Phase A
- **Phase D**: *Derive change requirements* – establish the gaps between the current architecture (from Phase B) and desired future architecture (from Phase C), and the resultant change-requirements and constraints in relation to the scope and business-issue (from Phase A)

By the end of Phase D we should have a set of business require-ments, which provide the *purpose* for subsequent solution-designs. Although technically speaking the architecture-assessment cycle doesn't complete until Phase H, the lessons-learned stage, the high-level architects drop back to a support-role at this point, handing over to the solution-architects. This second part of the cycle is much closer to the original TOGAF ADM: the only key differences are that, again, the project can be at any scale, and it can cover more than just an IT-centric scope:

- **Phase E**: *Design solutions* – work with solution-designers to assess options and trade-offs between requirements and constraints (from Phase D) to identify high-level solution-designs for the required changes

- **Phase F**: *Plan implementation* – work with governance, portfolio and change management teams to develop transformation blueprints, change-programmes and individual implementation-projects
- **Phase G**: *Guide implementation* – work with programme and project managers to assist in resolving trade-offs between architecture and implementation

When all projects arising from the assessment are complete, the high-level architects and solution-architects alike need to carry out a 'lessons learned' exercise, not only to identify any architectural concerns that might trigger new architecture-cycles, but also to review core definitions for the architecture itself: standards such as key components in the framework, the glossary and thesaurus, and even the underlying Architecture Charter.

- **Phase H**: *Review lessons-learned* – assess all issues arising from the architecture cycle, and identify (and, where appropriate, implement) any required changes to architecture standards and processes

The architecture is never 'complete': but it never pretends to be, either. Instead, it grows and changes with each iteration, creating a richer and more valuable view of the enterprise as a whole.

Dynamic architecture

There's an important complication here in that the architecture is necessarily *dynamic*. Architectural assessment may be quick, but implementation often is not, and the architecture may well have moved on by the time implementation catches up. So both the architecture cycle and the architecture itself need to be designed to work with this stark fact.

The problem is that most existing approaches describe an architecture in terms of a 'current-state' and a desired 'future-state'. We can just about get away with this for a simple narrow-scope IT-architecture; but the reality is that *nothing* is static, there *is* no 'state' – especially at the 'city-plan' level implied by true enterprise wide architecture. Everything depends on everything else, and everything is changing, at different speeds and in different ways. Complex, to say the least.

To support dynamics properly, we need a sophisticated system of versioning and prioritisation, with dependencies mapped to different versions as required. The catch is that whilst there's no doubt that we need a sophisticated toolset to manage all this complexity, none of the current crop of toolsets come anywhere close to what we actually need – see *Basics – artefacts and toolsets*, p.17. Some don't really handle versioning at all, whilst the only toolset with a halfway-decent versioning system has no scripting language, so we can't do much with the versioning anyway. And we need consistent versioning and mapping across *all* of the architecture repositories – not just modelling, but requirements, issues, compliance and everything else – so it doesn't actually help us if the requirements versioning is excellent and the model versioning all but non-existent, as is the case with one well-known toolset.

So until the toolset vendors wake up to the complexities of enterprise level architecture, we're still on our own to some extent in managing architecture dynamics. There *are* workarounds in every case, though inevitably all are somewhat labour-intensive and somewhat fragile; they also depend on the toolset in use, so I can't give specific advice here. The first and most important requirement, though, is simply to respect that complexity, design for it, work *with* it – and not hide from it in misleading terms such as 'future state'!

Application

- What formal methodology – if any – do you use for your current architecture?
- What are the boundaries of that methodology – for example, does its scope address only IT-systems or IT-services?
- How do you address architectural concerns beyond the nominal scope of the methodology?
- How do you address the dynamics of architecture – versions, interactions, lifecycles and so on – within the methodology?
- If you use an architecture toolset, in what ways does the toolset support or constrain the methodology?
- What processes and products are used for governance of that methodology?

Resources

TOGAF ADM: see www.opengroup.org/architecture/togaf8-doc/arch/toc.html (chapter 'Introduction to the ADM')

METHODOLOGY – PREPARATION

Summary

Before we conduct any business-critical architecture, we need to decide on and verify the details of the governance, framework and methodology we are to use. We also need to review this over-lighting structure on a regular basis, to ensure that it aligns with the changing needs of the enterprise.

Details

Preparation – an overview

In terms of the methodology, preparation for architecture consists of a single phase, described as 'Phase P'. In essence, this is a standard architecture cycle, but applied to the architecture itself – hence there's a strong emphasis on issues such as standards, principles and governance. It's also during this phase that we secure or renew essentials such as funding and authority from the executive to do the work.

Phase P – preliminaries

This phase is all about defining "how we do architecture". We identify the overall scope of enterprise-architecture, the authorisation from the executive to conduct enterprise-architecture, the architecture team and their roles, responsibilities and function within the organisation. It's also essential in this phase to outline the overall governance, frameworks and methodologies to be used for architecture development and architecture services.

> If you're familiar with TOGAF 8, most of this should be well-trodden territory. The main difference here is that we've merged much of TOGAF's 'Phase A' into this part of the process.
>
> The reason is that TOGAF 8 not only has a fixed scope, but also tends to do things in a big way: although in principle it's an iterative process, a typical TOGAF ADM cycle will take many months, if not years.
>
> In the original TOGAF ADM, the Preliminaries are all the governance things – Principles, Charter and so on – whilst Phase A sets up the fine details of the scope within the fixed TOGAF framework. In this revised

> ADM, though, we could be working with any scope, but more often
> small than large: a complete architecture iteration might take as little
> as a few hours in some cases, and still deliver business-usable results.
> So whilst the detail-scope parts of Phase A remain where they are, we
> move the definition of the overall framework, and operational setup,
> to become part of the preliminaries here, so that we have everything
> that we'll need already in place before we start any active architecture
> work.

Key products include the Architecture Charter, Architecture Principles and core high-level content for the architecture framework.

This phase is independent of the main architecture cycle. Since it provides oversight to the main cycle, we need to do it at least once before any architecture work takes place, but we also need to revisit it at regular intervals – for example, as a formal annual review.

Objectives, inputs and outputs

The objectives of the Preliminary Phase are:

- ensure that everyone who will be involved in, or benefit from, this approach is committed to the success of the architectural process;
- ensure that this evolution of architecture development has proper recognition and endorsement from corporate management, and the support and commitment of the necessary line management;
- validate the business principles, business goals, and strategic business drivers of the organisation;
- define architecture principles that will inform the constraints on any architecture work;
- define the organisation's 'architecture footprint' – the people responsible for doing the architecture work, where they're located, their responsibilities and so on;
- define the scope and assumptions (particularly if there's a 'federated architecture' to be shared with others);
- define the overall framework and working details of the methodologies that are to be used to develop architectures within the enterprise;
- evaluate and confirm the selection of architecture tools, repositories, and repository management processes that you will use to capture, publish, and maintain architecture artefacts;

- define the scope of the architecture effort, and identify and prioritise its components;
- identify the relevant stakeholders, and their concerns and objectives;
- identify the key business requirements for the current architecture effort, and any applicable constraints;
- secure resources and formal approval to do the work.

The inputs (▶) and outputs (◀) created in the Preliminary Phase are:

- ▶ Request for Architecture Work (p.172)
- ◀ Governance documents such as Architecture Charter (p.170), Architecture Governance (p.171), Architecture Principles (p.171), Architecture Standards (p.172)
- ◀ Architecture-models repository ('Enterprise Continuum') (p.179)
- ◀ Requirements repository (p.180)
- ◀ Glossary and thesaurus (p.182)
- ◀ Issues/ risks registers (p.180)
- ◀ Architecture-dispensations register (p.181)
- ◀ Phase-completion report – stakeholder review of preliminaries (p.177)

If a version of an output document already exists, it will be an input to the Phase, and may be amended during the Phase.

Steps

Typical steps include the following:

Step P1 – Establish the enterprise-architecture capability

Follow your own organisation's procedures to secure enterprise-wide recognition of the architecture capability; endorsement by corporate management to do the work, and to cross organisational boundaries where necessary; appropriate funding to establish and maintain the capability; and the support and commitment of any line management whose work would be affected by the architecture.

Include by reference the enterprise's governance framework, explaining how the architecture capability relates to that framework (for example, as a support function for an enterprise-wide programme-management office). Document this in the Architecture Governance document.

Under those governance rules, prepare a Request for Architecture Work that covers the scope and context for the remainder of the work for this Preliminary Phase.

If they don't already exist, create the required shared-information repositories:

- Architecture-models repository
- Requirements repository
- Issues register
- Risks / opportunities register
- Architecture-dispensations register
- Glossary and Thesaurus

> You're also going to need to set up an appropriate EA toolset as part of this process – which is not a quick or easy task, as most of the existing toolsets are insanely expensive, and still a long way from providing all of the functionality we need.
>
> As described earlier – see *Basics – artefacts and toolsets*, p.17 – you *can* sort-of get away with using Excel and Visio and the like for the first exploratory steps, but at some point you'll have to bite the bullet and obtain a proper purpose-built toolset. Not much fun, unfortunately, you'll discover soon enough that it *is* essential.

Record the results of this step in a preliminary draft (or review-draft) of the Architecture Charter document. (For the Preliminary Phase, the Architecture Charter acts as the equivalent of the Statement of Architecture Work – in other words a formal record of architectural decisions, actions and results.)

Step P2 – Identify Architecture Principles

Review the principles under which the enterprise architecture will be developed. Architecture principles are usually either based on or extensions of the core principles of the enterprise, including the organisation's Vision and Values. Ensure that any existing definitions are current and valid, and clarify any areas of ambiguity. Otherwise, go back to the responsible governance-body, and work with them to define these essential items from scratch and secure their endorsement by corporate management.

Record the agreed principles in the Architecture Principles document.

Amend the Architecture Charter document as appropriate, to reference the applicable principles and so on.

Step P3 – Identify applicable business policy, legislation and regulations

Review any policies and regulations, whether internal or external, which the enterprise-architecture capability must reflect and implement. Typical core policies include security policy, OH&S policy, privacy policy, environment policy, quality-system etc. Ensure that any existing definitions are still current and valid, and clarify any areas of ambiguity. Otherwise, go back to the respective bodies within the business, and work with them to resolve any issues and secure endorsement by corporate management.

Record the results of this step in the architecture-repository as entries in the 'Universals' layer of the framework

Amend the Architecture Charter document as appropriate, to reference the applicable policies and suchlike.

Step P4 – Identify applicable Standards

Repeat the above for any applicable Standards, whether internal or external, which the enterprise architecture capability must reflect and implement. If necessary, go back to the respective bodies within the business, and work with them to resolve any issues and secure endorsement by corporate management.

> Note that the framework and the structures and metamodels for each of the Enterprise Continuum repositories are also in effect Standards for your enterprise architecture, and need to be identified and managed as such here.

Record or reference the Standards in the Architecture Standards document. If appropriate, also create respective architecture-repository entries in the 'Universals' layer of the framework.

Amend the Architecture Charter document as appropriate, to reference the applicable Standards etc.

Step P5 – Identify core business-goals and business-drivers

Apply the same review-process with any core business goals and strategic drivers of the organisation which are deemed to apply for the time-periods covered by the architecture.

These should usually have already been defined elsewhere within the enterprise. If so, ensure that the definitions are still current and valid, and clarify any areas of ambiguity. Otherwise, go back to business groups responsible for definition of such goals and drivers and work with them to define these essential items from scratch and secure their endorsement by corporate management.

Record the results of this step in the architecture-repository as entries in the 'Universals' layer of the framework.

Step P6 – Identify enterprise-architecture scope

Define what is and isn't within the scope of the intended enterprise architecture capability. In particular, define:

- breadth of coverage of the enterprise
- applicable time horizons to be supported for 'future-context' assessments
- any architectural assets to be leveraged, or considered for use, from the organisation's Enterprise Continuum:
  - assets created in previous architecture efforts within the enterprise
  - assets available elsewhere in the industry (frameworks, systems models, vertical industry models, etc.)

From these, determine which overall architecture domains should be developed, to what level of detail, and which architecture views should be built. Ensure that the Architecture Repository includes metamodels – see *Framework – an overview*, p.53 – sufficient to cover all aspects and views for this scope.

Amend the Architecture Charter document as appropriate to describe or reference the applicable scope.

Step P7 – Identify constraints

Identify the operational constraints that must be addressed, including enterprise-wide constraints and any architecture-specific constraints such as time, schedule, resources, etc. The enterprise-wide constraints may be informed by the business-principles and architecture principles developed in the steps above.

Amend the Architecture Charter document as appropriate, to reference the applicable constraints.

Step P8 – Identify stakeholders and concerns, business requirements, and overall architecture Vision

Identify key stakeholders and their concerns and objectives; define the key business requirements to be addressed in this overall architecture effort; and articulate an Architecture Vision that will address those requirements, within the defined scope and constraints, conforming with the business and architecture principles.

Record the concerns and requirements, and their respective stakeholders, as entries in the Requirements Repository. (If requirements are maintained within the architecture repository, record the requirements as entries in the 'Why' [reasons / decisions] column of the framework.)

Amend the Architecture Charter document as appropriate, to reference the applicable stakeholders and the overall Architecture Vision for the current development.

Step P9 – Identify content for high-level models

Use the core-principles, scope, requirements, constraints and the like from the above steps to suggest candidate items for each cell in the 'Planner' (row-1) layer of the framework:

- *what*: key data-items, key physical 'things' etc
- *how*: key processes, functions etc
- *where*: key locations, physical, virtual etc
- *who*: key capabilities, actors/agents, organisations etc
- *when*: key events, cycles etc
- *why*: key continuing aims, strategies etc

Record the results in the respective sections of the architecture-repository. Depending on the capabilities of the toolset, these may be in either list- or graphic-form, but it must be possible to link to these from other layers of the stored framework.

Note that in the first pass through the Preliminary Phase, you may only have minimal content to store, but you'll add further content during architecture cycles and subsequent Preliminary Phase reviews.

Step PX – Secure approval for Architecture Charter, governance, etc

Estimate the resources you'll need to operate the architecture capability. If it's a new capability – for example, if this is the first time you've done a Preliminary Phase – develop a roadmap and schedule for the proposed development; otherwise identify the existing resources and any changes required for the period under review

Amend the Architecture Charter to include these items, usually by reference.

Secure formal approval of the Architecture Charter under the ap-propriate governance procedures. Once you've done this, the Architecture Charter, together with the applicable documents for Principles, Governance, Standards and so on, will act as the formal authority to conduct architecture work as subsequent iter-ations through the Phase A to Phase H cycle.

Application

- What methodology do you use at present for architecture?
- What processes does it provide for preparation for architecture?
- What formal process – if any – do you use for managing, reviewing and updating the methodology itself?
- In what ways – if any – is the current architecture linked to the high-level 'universals' of the enterprise?
- What is the current scope and authority for 'enterprise architecture'? Under whose governance? If it does not have a true enterprise-wide scope and authority, what would need to change in order to attain these?

Resources

TOGAF and ADM preliminary phases: see www.opengroup.org/architecture/togaf8-doc/arch/toc.html (chapters 'Preliminary Phase: Framework and Principles' and 'Phase A: Architecture Vision')

METHODOLOGY – ASSESSMENT

Summary

The first half of the architecture-cycle is focussed on structure and high-level design: 'architecture proper'. Starting with a business need, we explore impacts and options, and derive requirements for change – adding to our knowledge of the enterprise structure as we do so.

Details

Assessment phases – an overview

It's in the assessment phases – Phases A to D of the architecture-cycle – that we create most of what other people would see as 'architecture': the models and design-requirements and suchlike. There's also a strong emphasis here on the link between methodology and the content and maintenance of the architecture framework.

If you're familiar with TOGAF, you'll need to do a slight readjustment in your thinking here. In principle it's much the same, but we do things in a different order, and often much more quickly than in the original ADM. We'll also have done some of the preliminary work already, so Phase A here has a slightly different emphasis and function.

The big change is that we don't assume TOGAF's fixed scope in each Phase, as 'Business Architecture' (original Phase B), 'Information-Systems Architecture' (original Phases C1 and C2) and 'Technology Architecture' (original Phase D). Instead, we allow an architecture cycle to have *any* scope – and we define that in the revised Phase A.

In the original ADM, we would do a separate as-is, to-be and gap-analysis in each Phase – which made sense there, because the predefined scope for each of their Phases would typically involve different stakeholders. But here we'll typically expect to engage the same stakeholders all the way through, so it makes more sense to split the work on the time-horizon boundaries instead.

If you want to use this variant to do 'classic' TOGAF-style IT-architecture, think of that as three distinct, successive passes through the revised assessment-Phases A to D. One pass has a 'Business Architecture' scope (typically higher-level Zachman); one has an 'Information-Systems Architecture' scope (typically mid-level Zachman, and possibly split in two for a separate Applications scope around *capability* and *function*, and a Data scope around *asset* » virtual); and the last has a 'Technology Architecture' scope (mostly low-level Zachman around *asset* and *location*). You'd then bring all of these together in an additional Phase D that merges and cross-compares all the different gap-analyses, leading on to the solution-phases in the usual way with a single Phase E. The original ADM does allow you to go back and forth in this way anyway: it's just that here we can be a bit more explicit about it, and do it under more explicit governance.

Not recommended to do it all in one go, though – it's all too big to be workable in practice, as many enterprise-architecture teams have found to their cost. It's much simpler, and much more reliable, to do it in smaller, more manageable chunks, each directly linked to an identifiable business need. But if the business really do insist that they want the classic 'big bang', there's nothing here that would stop you from doing so – go right ahead, and have fun as best you can, perhaps?

Since architectural design is the centre of attention here, rather than the details of implementation, the focus of governance is more on the architecture itself than programme-management – though the latter should at least be informed, and preferably engaged, in every step of the process.

Phase A – establish iteration scope

This phase is the start-point of a regular architectural-services cycle.

During this phase we work with whoever's sponsoring the architecture cycle to identify the purpose, scope and context of the iteration.

The main output of this phase is the *Statement of Architecture Work*, which guides the subsequent phases of the cycle.

Objectives, inputs and outputs

The objectives of Phase A are:

- define the key business requirements to be addressed in this cycle, and any constraints that must be addressed;
- define the scope of the iteration, and identify and prioritise its components;
- identify the relevant stakeholders, and their concerns and objectives;
- identify applicable business principles, goals, strategic drivers and the like for this iteration;
- understand the impact on, and of, other enterprise architecture development-cycles going on in parallel;

- ensure that this iteration has proper authority of the respective corporate and/or line management;
- secure resources and formal approval to proceed.

The inputs (▶, or ▲ indicates input may also be changed) and outputs (◀) are:

▶ Request for Architecture Work (p.172)
▲ Architecture-models repository (p.179)
▲ Requirements repository (p.180)
▲ Glossary and thesaurus (p.182)
▲ Issues / risks registers (p.180)
▶ Architecture-dispensations register (p.181)
◀ Statement of Architecture Work (as phase-completion report) (p.174)

Steps

Typical steps include the following:

Step A1 – Establish the business-purpose and scope of the cycle

Identify the purpose and scope of the architecture cycle. (This should have been documented in the Request for Architecture Work which initiates the architecture cycle with this Phase, but you may need to develop it together with the sponsor.)

The purpose should always be described in *business* terms – see *Purpose – business-driven architecture*, p.29 – and should not pre-suppose any particular solution. Examples include:

- *improved effectiveness*: for example, review of a project's compliance with current or future architecture, to optimise cost-savings overall
- *process reengineering*: for example, exploration of the full trail of interactions of an end-to-end process triggered by one or more client-types
- *strategy-assessment*: strategic analysis of potential impact of a change in technology, legislation etc
- *risk-assessment*: for example, analysis of the impact of a potential or actual failure of a single component – such as a server, router or cable-connection – or the unavailability of a facility due to fire or flood

One of the most common enterprise-architecture mistakes that IT-architects tend to make is what we might call "IT solution looking for enterprise problem" – in traditional terms, putting the cart before the horse. To resolve this, we insist that anything that looks like a solution is shelved until Phase E in the architecture-cycle – otherwise we end up confusing would-be 'solutions' with real requirements.

During a recent training-session, for example, an IT-architect asked us how we would use the methodology to assess the impact of implementing Microsoft SharePoint. Starting at Phase A, we immediately parked SharePoint itself as a potential solution for Phase E, and asked for the *business* requirement for which it was a solution – a question to which the response was an interesting silence. "Well, it's for online collaboration…", was the eventual answer. Fine, that's a kind of solution too, so let's put that in Phase E as well: and what's the underlying business requirement for 'online collaboration'? "Uh… collaboration in general, I suppose?" That *was* a real business-issue for the client: but it wasn't where he'd started.

In effect, he'd started from a 'solution', had tried to implement it without any *apparent* business-requirement, and then wondered why he couldn't find a business sponsor to fund it – in other words, trying to run the architecture process back-to-front. By withholding on 'solutions' in Phase A, and instead repeatedly pushing back and back to the core business need, we were able to identify a number of collaboration issues that had genuine meaning to the business. As it happened, the analysis in Phase E *did* show that implementing SharePoint was a good solution for their business-problems around collaboration – but as part of a much broader portfolio of business-oriented changes, rather than as an indefensible, standalone 'solution looking for a problem'.

Define what is inside and outside the scope of the cycle's architecture effort. In particular, identify:

- breadth of coverage of the enterprise for the cycle;
- level of detail to be defined;
- specific architecture domains to be covered (for example, for an IT-centric project, the Business, Data, Applications and Technology domains);
- locations in time of any required 'to-be' time-horizons;
- architectural assets to be leveraged, or considered for use, from the organisation's Enterprise Continuum

Record the results of this step in a preliminary draft of the Statement of Architecture Work for the cycle.

Step A2 – *Review applicable Architecture Principles, policies etc*

Review the high-level principles, policies, legislation and regulation which would apply to the scope for the architecture-cycle. These principles are usually derived from or based on the Principles and policies identified in the Preliminary Phase.

As in the Preliminary Phase, ensure that the existing definitions are still current and valid, and clarify any areas of ambiguity. If not, work with the sponsor to define these items and, if necessary, secure their endorsement by corporate management.

Amend the Statement of Architecture Work to reference the applicable Principles and so on.

Step A3 – Identify business goals and strategic drivers

Do the same with the strategic drivers and high-level business goals for the cycle. These should build on or devolve from the goals and drivers of the organisation, as identified in the Preliminary Phase.

As in step A2, ensure these are current and valid; if not, define or update them, and obtain any necessary formal endorsement for the changes.

Amend the Statement of Architecture Work to reference the applicable goals and drivers.

Step A4 – Establish the architecture-framework scope of the cycle

Using the business-purpose, business-scope, principles and drivers identified above, establish the applicable scope in terms of the architecture framework's layers, columns, segments and cells – see *Framework – layers*, p. 59, *Framework – primitives*, p.63 and *Framework – composites*, p.79.

> With very few exceptions, the real-world consists of composites that straddle across all or part of the bottommost row of the framework, the 'Operations' layer. Everything else that we deal with in architecture is a literally 'un-realistic' abstraction.
>
> To guide our sense-making and redesign, we need to end up with abstractions such as the 'architectural primitives' of the framework: but we always *start* from the composites in the real world – all the things that we see, we touch, with which we interact.
>
> So to identify scope, we need to take those composites apart – identify the primitive 'atoms' behind the composites' 'compounds'. This also helps to identify the models we'll need when we get deeper into the architectural assessment in Phase B and Phase C.
>
> Most domain-architecture seems to consist of assembling ready-made components into a different order. So this process may at first seem somewhat counter-intuitive, because in a sense we're running the usual design process backwards, from complete design back to components.
>
> We also need to be wary of falling back into the language of the 'engineering the enterprise' metaphor – as I've just done above, in fact. In the 'living enterprise', everything is always connected to everything else; the real scope here is *always* 'the everything'. For sanity's sake, we apply artificial bounds to the scope here, by working backwards from the items that appear to be in scope; but it's important to keep in mind that we may well need to extend that scope at any time.

Identify the applicable layers (vertical scope) for the iteration from the business-purpose – for example:

- *improved effectiveness*: usually R2 ('business') to R4 ('develop')
- *process reengineering*: usually R3 ('system') to R5 ('implement')
- *strategy-assessment*: R2 or even R1 ('scope') for a major change, to R4, R5 or even R6 ('operations')
- *risk-assessment*: usually from R6 or R5 *upward* to R3, or even R2 for impacts on high-level performance-criteria

For each column, in each framework-row in scope for the cycle:

- identify the applicable 'slice' (level of detail)
- identify the applicable 'sliver' (coverage across organisation)
- identify 'the applicable segment' (categories of items covered)

The 'architectures' in conventional frameworks such as TOGAF and FEAF are predefined framework-scopes – in other words pre-packaged sets of 'slices' and 'segments', usually only within an IT-centric 'sliver' of the organisation. These 'architectures' or *views* emphasise different areas of the framework:

- *Business Architecture* (TOGAF Phase B): emphasis on R2 'conceptual' layer
- *Data Architecture* (TOGAF Phase C1) and *Application Architecture* (TOGAF Phase C2): emphasis on R3 'logical' layer
- *Technology Architecture* (TOGAF Phase D): emphasis on R4 'physical' layer

Although we can use such predefined views in some cases, a better approach in this step is to identify the required scope from the context of the purpose, and in turn derive the applicable views from the scope. For example, compare the different 'slices' for the views of data architecture and information-architecture:

- *data-architecture*:
  - explore 'What » virtual' (data) column/segment in full depth from R1 to R4
  - limited interest in any other column/segment in any row
- *information-architecture*:
  - explore 'What » virtual' (i.e. data) column/segment in full depth from R1 to R3, with some depth in R4
  - explore intersection of 'What » virtual' and '» relational' (i.e. narrative-knowledge) column/segment, with same slices

- explore intersection of 'What » virtual' / '» relational' with 'Why' column (i.e. derivation of information from data) with same slices
- explore intersection across all of R3 'logical' layer (e.g. processes, events etc significant to information-gathering), usually in somewhat less detail

Amend the Statement of Architecture Work to record the applicable framework-scope.

Step A5 – Identify additional stakeholders, concerns and requirements

To identify other potential stakeholders in the cycle's architecture, search the architecture-repository for business-owners of items within the scope identified in the previous step. Review the issues-, risks- and architecture-dispensation registers for other potential stakeholders whose concerns may be impacted by the project. Use trails of connections within the repository to identify further concerns and objectives.

Identify additional business requirements that may be applicable to the respective architecture-scope. If appropriate, create a context-specific section of the requirements-repository to hold these requirements, in accordance with the project- or programme-management rules specified in the Architecture Charter.

Amend the Statement of Architecture Work as appropriate to record these additional items.

Step A6 – Identify additional constraints

Identify any additional constraints that must be addressed, including enterprise-wide constraints and project-specific constraints (time, schedule, resources, etc.). The enterprise-wide constraints may be informed by the business and architecture principles developed in the Preliminary Phase or clarified as part of this Phase.

Amend the Statement of Architecture Work as appropriate to record these additional items.

Step AX – Secure approval for Statement of Architecture Work

Based on the purpose, focus, scope, constraints, etc, define a project-plan for the cycle – in other words, a set of architecture activities that will address the requirements, within the defined scope and constraints, and conforming with the business and architecture principles. Estimate the resources needed, and, for a larger project, develop a roadmap and schedule for the proposed development. Document all of these items in the Statement of Architecture Work for the project, and present for formal review.

After the stakeholder review, secure formal approval of the Statement of Architecture Work under appropriate governance procedures, to begin the architecture analysis.

Phase B – assess current context

This phase establishes the current context – in other words, the 'as-is' status – for the scope specified in Phase A for this architectural cycle. This includes an assessment of impact of qualitative criteria such as performance, cost, confidentiality, security, reliability, service-levels, etc; and of whole-of-organisation impact, where one part of the architecture may need to change to cater for changes in another part of the overall architecture.

During this Phase, you'll create models and views to describe this 'as-is' context, in some cases drawing upon models already created for the respective project. In earlier stages of architectural development, it's likely you'll add new content to the shared architecture-models repository, to record additional information about the overall architectural context for the organisation elicited during the assessment for this architecture-cycle's scope.

Any requirements, issues and risks identified during the assessment should be added to the respective repository or register.

A stakeholder review of the current-context architecture will be conducted at the end of this phase.

Objectives, inputs and outputs

The objectives of Phase B are:

- describe the 'as-is' architecture for the scope of defined by the Statement of Architecture Work;
- select relevant architecture viewpoints that will enable the architect to demonstrate how the stakeholder concerns are addressed in the overall architecture;
- select the relevant tools and techniques to be used in association with the selected viewpoints.

The inputs (▶, ▲) and outputs (◀) are:

- ▲ Statement of Architecture Work (p.174)
- ▶ Project- and/or context-specific documents from other sources
- ▲ Architecture-models repository (p.179)
- ▲ Requirements repository (p.180)

► Glossary and thesaurus (p.182)

▲ Issues / risks registers (p.180)

► Architecture-dispensations register (p.181)

◄ Architecture models (published as required)

◄ Phase-completion report – stakeholder review of current architecture (p.177)

Steps

Typical steps include the following:

Step B1 – Develop Baseline Architecture for 'as-is' context

Identify any primitives, composites, models and other artefacts that may already exist in the architecture-references for the scope specified in Phase A. These references include:

- architecture-repository
- requirements repository
- risks register
- issues register
- dispensations register
- glossary and thesaurus

As appropriate, create views and models from these artefacts to describe the current scope – in other words, a summary of what is already known about the current 'as-is' context implied by these artefacts. This represents the architectural baseline for the scope prior to the analysis.

> Most of the current toolsets are not good at handling the uncertainties of work-in-progress. If that's the case for yours, it's a good idea to create an iteration-specific view into the architecture repository – a 'project encyclopaedia', or whatever the equivalent term is for your toolset. In general, use a separate encyclopaedia whenever an assessment is likely to create new architectural-primitives or composites.
>
> This temporary encyclopaedia should be used to document all development work for each Phase of the current architecture-cycle. You can then merge appropriate parts of this content back into the main repository after each end-of-phase review, though the main merge won't take place until the end of Phase H, the end-of-cycle lessons-learned review.

Record the resultant descriptions and models in appropriate forms for later review.

Step B2 – Select reference-models, views and viewpoints

Using the baseline-architecture as a guide, identify any reference-models that apply to the iteration-scope. These models would guide or mandate specific items for compliance purposes in the context: for example, use of a particular protocol, technology, operating system, etc.

In the architecture-repository, these will typically be derived from the upper layers – rows R1 to R3 – though in a few cases, particularly for technical compliance, reference-models may even apply down to R5. The references should always include any overarching enterprise-wide Principles, Standards and the like from the R0 'Universals' row, as identified during Phase A.

Use the Request for Architecture Work (as referenced in or incorporated into the Statement of Architecture Work) to identify appropriate viewpoints, such as Security, Operations, Finance, and specific client-groups.

Identify tools, techniques and model-types that match the required scope for the architecture-cycle, and support the required views and viewpoints. Use the mappings between framework rows, columns and segments and model-types to assist in this.

Step B3 – Create and update 'as-is' architecture models

Identify any additional reference-materials for the iteration-scope, such as:

- project documents – requirements, process-models, database schemas
- external project-specific standards and constraints – such as technology standards, vendor specifications etc

Using these references, and the viewpoints, tools, techniques and model-types selected in the previous steps, expand the baseline architecture into a comprehensive architecture for the iteration context, to the level of detail and organisational breadth as specified in the full scope in the Statement of Architecture Work.

To do this, scan through the scope of the framework, at the level of detail specified in the Statement of Architecture Work for each row, column and segment, to identify appropriate primitives and composites.

> We scan through the framework in a systematic way here because it's the anchor for the architecture repository and categorisation of models. The scope for this iteration should already have been defined in framework terms during Phase A.

This step (and the matching step in Phase C) is where most of the model-creation takes place. Model-types should have been linked to framework cells via the underlying root-primitives for each entity-type in the model, so identifying a framework cell automatically implies a set of model-types or views that may be appropriate for the context.

In our own architecture practice, we parallel this activity with a range of other methodologies, particularly Viable Services modelling – see 'Integration – the service-oriented enterprise' in *Framework – integration*, p.99; the VPEC-T methodology (values, process, events, content, trust); SqEME process modelling; and causal layered analysis. We'll also include some of our own home-grown techniques, such as enterprise effectiveness modelling and whole-of-enterprise architecture. More detail on those from the links in the *Resources* section at the end of the chapter.

In principle the scan through the framework could be done in any order, though the typical approach is top-down, from R0 to R6:

- scan *down* rows to identify composites and their underlying primitives
- for each identified item in the current row, column and segment
  - o review its links from and/or to primitives in the row(s) above
  - o links and derivations may be in other columns – for example, business-processes implied by business-principles, or '‹implements›' links to business-requirements
    - o note that it may be necessary to create primitives in rows above if the required items to link to do not exist
  - o look in the row below for implied primitives and composites
    - o conceptual-to-logical example: logical data-entities implied by business-data object
    - o logical-to-physical example: implied physical cross-reference table to implement logical many-to-many data-relationship
- identify and document the owners and stakeholders for the item
- check and validate its links to *all* R0 items (vision, values, principles, standards etc)
- scan *across* rows and/or segments to identify multi-cell composites

- o examples: business-patterns; business-unit maps; actors, business-functions, events, data and objects in process-models
    - o note that a primitive might be expressed only as a composite in a lower row
- use the selected model-types to create and document relationship-links:
  - o same-type relationships between primitives
  - o note that some model-types consist of related primitives (i.e. of the same general item-type) linked downward through a single column
    - o examples: data entity-relationship model, functional decomposition, parts-breakdown
  - o same model-type relationships between composites
    - o example: end-to-end process-chain
  - o membership of primitives in composites
    - o implied automatically in creating the respective model
  - o complex relationships between primitives and composites
    - o examples: derivation-trail for information-model; '‹implements›' links between data, processes and business-requirements

Although the top-down approach above is recommended for general architectural analysis – such as for business-process re-engineering or strategic impact-analysis – other approaches may be more useful for other contexts, for example:

- *risk-analysis or failure-analysis for implementation-level components*:
  - o identify the component
    - o examples: application-server, router, cable-connection
  - o identify the framework row, column(s) and segment(s) for the individual component
  - o component may be either primitive or composite
    - o example: cable-connection is a composite – physical object plus locations
  - o real components are usually at R6 implementation-level
  - o move upward to identify higher-level aggregations which use the component
  - o move downward again from those aggregations, to identify other implementation-level components which may be affected by the risk or failure

- o repeat upward to explore impact on all related higher-row aggregations and their associated implementations as required
  - o example: R6 component-failure may impact R2 business-performance metric
- *resolve a business 'pain-point':*
  - o use the description of the pain-point – to identify the start-point in the framework
    - o example: issues around a misleading performance-indicator suggest logical-layer data – hence a start-point of R3 ('logical'), 'What » virtual' (data)
  - o work outwards in any direction (upwards, downwards, sideways) from that point
  - o identify trails of connections between primitives and composites that aggregate (upward) or implement (downward) a related item
  - o identify items or connections that appear to be implied but are missing from the model and/or the context

Document the results of the analysis as primitives, composites and models in the respective encyclopaedia in the architecture repository, and, if appropriate, as requirements or constraints in the requirements repository, or as risks or issues in the respective register.

Step B4 – Review 'as-is' architecture against qualitative criteria

Identify the qualitative criteria that will apply for the context of the architecture cycle, such as performance, costs, volumes etc:

- Zachman also suggests the following qualitative concerns to match each framework column:
  - o *what* (asset): inventory-management
  - o *how* (function): yield-management
  - o *where* (location): capacity-management
  - o *who* (capability): performance-management
  - o *when* (event): time-management
  - o *why* (decision): state-of-change management
- include all applicable R0 'Universals'
  - o examples: security, environment, OH&S, ethics, and any other 'pervasive services' in the service-oriented enterprise

- other examples of qualitative criteria might include sets of key performance-indicators (KPIs) and critical success-factors (CSFs) for a Balanced Scorecard

Ensure that the 'as-is' architecture for the context appropriately describes and implements each of these qualitative criteria. Amend the architecture design as necessary to satisfy these implied requirements.

Document in the respective repositories and registers any changes indicated by the review.

Step B5 – Finalise building-blocks for the architectural scope

Identify applicable primitives and composites that have potential for re-use or compliance, or have already been flagged as such.

Architectural Building Blocks (ABBs)

Primitives and (with some care) root-composites may be flagged as what TOGAF describes as 'Architectural Building Blocks' – root-level architectural items which must, should or could be re-used in specific contexts. ABBs are usually members of some kind of Architectural Reference Model: their use in the architecture supports consistency through compliance.

> For practical reasons – simply because many true primitives are too abstract to make business sense on their own – it may be appropriate to also class as ABBs some of the base-level composites (see *Framework – composites*, p.79). Be careful to label them accordingly, though, or else you may find yourself in difficulty when redesigns have to go right down to the roots, as in some types of security analysis and disaster-recovery planning.

There's a balance needed between conformity and flexibility in different designs, which can be achieved by varying the extent to which ABBs are considered to be binding (see 'Composites and 'completeness'' in *Framework – composites*, p.85). Higher-level items – from higher rows on the framework – are usually 'mandatory' or 'highly desirable' by definition, because high bindedness at a lower level automatically implies equivalent or higher bindedness in any items in rows above to which it is linked. Variations in bindedness are most common in R3 'Logical' and R4 'Physical' layers, but in some cases items may even be mandatory as low as R5 'Implementation'. Note too that *all ABBs are abstract*: the moment we identify a specific, concrete item, it becomes an SBB for solution-design, not an ABB for architecture. For example:

- *R3, recommended*: data-designs should build on an industry-standard logical data-model, extending those designs only where essential
- *R4, mandatory*: all desktop-computer systems must run the Standard Operating Environment (a set of software capabilities – i.e. 'Who » virtual' items)
- *R4, recommended*: project-management functions should comply with the specified standards
- *R4, desirable*: software-implementation designs should use a specific framework (i.e. 'Who » virtual' again)
- *R5, suggested*: the customer-services switchboard is the appropriate contact-point for most types of general enquiry (i.e. referenced as either a location and/or as a capability)
- *R5, mandatory*: in the event of system failure, the designated fallback router shall be used

In general, bindedness of ABBs at R5 is more an operational issue than an architectural one, but becomes architecturally relevant in risk-analysis, failure-analysis and some types of system design and process reengineering.

Amend the documentation of ABBs in the respective encyclo-paedia to record the selected degree of bindedness for each.

Solution Building Blocks (SBBs)

Composites of any type and at any level may be flagged as Solution Building Blocks (to again use the TOGAF term). These identify proven patterns in which the ABBs in Reference Models can be applied successfully in practice; they also support effectiveness and comprehensibility through re-use of solution designs. SBBs are often layered, with higher-level SBB patterns constructed of lower-level SBBs and ABBs, and may have the same levels of 'bindedness' as for ABBs:

- *mandatory*: must use
- *recommended*: should use
- *desirable*: advised to use
- *suggested*: could use

Potential SBBs will present as re-usable patterns or structures, usually across a single framework row, sometimes also down framework columns. For example:

- *high-level process* – pattern of What, How, Where and Who
- *many-to-many data-relationship* – pattern of 'What » virtual' (data) in R3 'Logical' and R4 'Physical' rows

- *organisational hierarchy* – multi-row recursive pattern of Where (location) and/or Who (role) at higher levels, expanding to 'What » relational' (explicit person) and/or How (function) at lower levels
- *'object factory' software-pattern* – R3 to R4 pattern of How (function) and Who (capability)

At the lower levels, SBBs often masquerade as apparent ABBs – a risk in itself, as SBBs are not requirements as such, but identified *solutions* to architectural requirements. In general, such 'pseudo-ABBs' should only be mandatory at low levels, as applications of an implementation specific Technical Reference Model. Examples include:

- *computer operating-system* (e.g. Unix/Linux) – pattern of 'How' (function) and 'Who » virtual' (software capability)
- *specified vendor for hardware type* (e.g. Dell for file-servers) – pattern of 'How' (function), 'What » physical' (object) and 'What » relational' (vendor)

The simplest means to identify pseudo-ABBS is to note that SBBs are composites, not primitives: if the item straddles across columns or rows or segments, it is a composite, and cannot be binding in the same way as an ABB.

It's important to understand that SBBs are useful *constraints* – not requirements, but context-specific *implementations* of underlying requirements. In effect, they are a type of generic Dispensation. The danger is that if pseudo-ABBs are misinterpreted as true ABBs, those constraints could be treated as genuine business-requirements in future designs – which, over time, would all but guarantee inappropriate or ineffective solutions. *Every SBB should be subject to regular review*, exactly as for all other Dispensations.

In all cases, identify and document any potential ABBs that occur as components in SBBs.

Amend the documentation of SBBs and any amended ABBs in the respective encyclopaedia to record the selected degree of binded-ness for each.

Step BX – Conduct checkpoint-review for stakeholders

Identify the stakeholders who need to be engaged in the architecture review, from the iteration-scope as specified in Phase A and the business-owners of additional items identified or developed in the previous steps of this Phase. Use a RACI matrix – see *RACI, CRUD and other matters*, p.44 – to identify the type and level of engagement.

136

Collate the results of the previous steps for stakeholder review:

- baseline
- reference-models
- context-models (primitives, relationships, composites)
- building-blocks (ABBs, SBBs)
- any additional risks, issues, requirements etc identified during the analysis

Present the results to the stakeholders for formal review under the governance procedures. Document the results of the review in a phase-completion-report.

As advised by the stakeholders, you might also amend the *Statement of Architecture Work* as appropriate to carry forward additional content and/or issues for subsequent phases of the architecture cycle – for example, suggested solutions (Phase E), suggested project structures (Phase F), potential architectural issues during implementation (Phase G), or notes for future architectural reviews (Phase H).

Merge the content of any project-specific encyclopaedia back into the current-context segment of the architecture repository, in accordance with the repository governance procedures.

Phase C – assess future context

This phase establishes the probable and/or intended future context – in other words, a 'to-be' architecture – for the scope and time-horizon specified in Phase A for this cycle. The review includes an assessment of impact of qualitative criteria such as performance, cost, confidentiality, security, reliability, service-levels, etc; and of whole-of-organisation impact, where one part of the architecture may need to change to cater for changes in another part of the overall architecture. (You may need to repeat this process multiple times for the same nominal scope if 'transitional states' for intermediate time horizons are required.)

A quick glance ahead will show you that Phase C looks a lot like Phase B – so much so that there's very little extra detail here.

That's deliberate: it isn't a mistake. The whole point here is to use a consistent approach, regardless of the context: so the only thing that should change in scope is the time-horizon, from 'as-is' to 'to-be'. If you find that anything else does change – for example, exploring the 'to-be' forces you to consider a wider scope in framework terms – it might be wise to review the results of Phase B, and if appropriate revisit that analysis to address the revised scope. It's essential that you

> compare like with like between Phase B and here, so that the
> subsequent gap-analysis in Phase D can make meaningful sense.

As in Phase B, you'll create models and views to describe this context. It's likely that you'll add new content to the shared architecture-models repository, to record additional information about the overall architectural context for the organisation and respective time-horizon(s) that is elicited during the assessment for the architecture-cycle's scope.

Any requirements, issues and risks identified during the assessment should be added to the respective repository or register.

A stakeholder review of the future-state architecture(s) should be conducted at the end of this phase.

Objectives, inputs and outputs

The objectives of Phase C include:

- develop one or more 'to-be' architectures for the scope and context of the iteration, describing product and/or service strategy, and organisational, functional, process, information, geographic or any other appropriate aspects of the business environment, based on the business principles, business goals, and strategic drivers

The inputs (►,▲) and outputs (◄) are:

- ► Statement of Architecture Work (p.174)
- ► Project- and/or context-specific documents from other sources
- ▲ Architecture-models repository (p.179)
- ▲ Requirements repository (p.180)
- ► Glossary and thesaurus (p.182)
- ▲ Issues / risks registers (p.180)
- ► Architecture-dispensations register (p.181)
- ◄ Architecture models (published as required)
- ◄ Phase-completion report – stakeholder review of future architecture (p.177)

Steps

The steps in Phase C are almost identical to those in Phase B: the only difference should be that the architecture developed should apply to the respective 'to-be' time-horizon rather than the current 'as-is'.

All steps other than the last – i.e. CX, the final stakeholder-review – should be repeated for each time-horizon in scope. The stakeholder review should cover and compare all future-context 'to-be' architectures developed in this Phase.

Step C1 – Develop Baseline Architecture for 'to-be' context

Create a baseline-architecture for the specific time-horizon, as described in Step B1.

If appropriate, create a project-specific encyclopaedia for this purpose. A separate encyclopaedia should be used for *each* 'to-be' time horizon in scope.

Step C2 – Select reference-models, views and viewpoints

Select appropriate reference-models, views and viewpoints into the architecture for the specific time-horizon, as described in Step B2.

These should be the same as in Phase B unless the reference-models are required to change for the respective time-horizons – for example, if a key technology or business-process is scheduled to change in the intervening period.

Step C3 – Create and update 'to-be' architecture models

Using the baseline-architecture from step C1, the reference-models, views and viewpoints selected in step C2, and any additional context-specific reference-information, develop a 'to-be' architecture for the respective time-horizon, as described in Step B3. Note also the impact of any relevant dispensations in the dispensations-register. Identify and document the resultant primitives, composites, models, requirements, issues and risks.

Step C4 – Review 'to-be' architecture against qualitative criteria

Review the 'to-be' architecture design against the selected qualitative criteria, as described in Step B4. In general, the set of criteria used should be the same for the 'as-is' context assessed in Phase B and in all 'to-be' contexts assessed in this Phase.

Step C5 – Finalise building-blocks for the architectural scope

Identify and document Architectural Building Blocks and Solution Building Blocks for the respective time-horizon, as described in Step B5.

Step CX – Conduct checkpoint-review for stakeholders

Identify the stakeholders for the scope, as described in Step BX. Note that some stakeholders may be different from those of Phase B, as a result of scheduled changes or altered impact-scopes for the future-state time-horizons.

Collate the results of the previous steps, for *each* time-horizon in scope, and present these to the stakeholders for formal review under the governance procedures. Document the results of the review in a phase-completion-report. As advised by the stakeholders, you might also amend the *Statement of Architecture Work* to carry forward additional content and/or issues for subsequent phases of the architecture cycle.

Merge the content of any project-specific encyclopaedias back into the respective 'to-be' segments of the architecture repository, in accordance with the repository governance procedures.

Phase D – derive change-requirements

This phase establishes the gap between the current 'as-is' context and the probable and/or intended future 'to-be' context(s) for the scope and time-horizon(s) specified in Phase A for this architectural cycle. Each gap highlights requirements for solutions and project- or migration-plans to manage the required change.

Typical architecture-gaps include:

- people gaps (e.g. availability, skill-sets, training, etc)
- process gaps (e.g. process handovers, scheduling, etc)
- tools gaps (e.g. equipment, duplicate or missing tool functionality)
- data gaps (e.g. not located where it is needed, not the data that is needed, not available when needed, etc)
- information gaps (e.g. inappropriate, incomplete or ambiguous mappings between data and business-rules)
- measurement gaps (e.g. missing metrics, measurement from inappropriate sources or via inappropriate transforms, etc)
- financial gaps (e.g. funding, schedules, etc)
- facilities gaps (e.g. buildings, work-space, infrastructure, energy-supply, etc.)
- security gaps (e.g. processes, people-interactions, systems etc)
- dependency gaps (e.g. in process implementations, quality-management, etc)
- value gaps (e.g. in value-chains and value-webs)
- meaning gaps (e.g. inappropriate Cynefin-style skill-level applied in a step for derivation of meaning

The aim of gap-analysis is to identify services, functions, data-elements, capabilities, applications and the like which may have been left out accidentally, deliberately eliminated, or are yet to be developed or procured.

> In particular, watch for stakeholder concerns that have not been addressed in previous architecture-work. If any of your stakeholders are upset or annoyed, there's usually a good reason, though sometimes it may not be obvious even to them as to what that reason may be!

The review should also assess impacts of qualitative criteria such as performance, cost, confidentiality, security, reliability and service-levels; and whole-of-organisation impact, where one part of the architecture may need to change to cater for changes in another part of the overall architecture. Where so-called 'transitional states' for intermediate time-horizons are required, you'll usually need to repeat this process for each 'as-is' / 'to-be' pair in the same nominal scope.

The primary output will be a set of change-requirements, though you'll sometimes also create models and views to describe the required transitions and system-changes. On occasion you'll also add new content to the shared architecture-models repository, to record additional information about the overall architectural context for the respective time-horizon(s) that you've elicited during gap-analysis for the iteration scope.

Any additional requirements, issues and risks identified during the assessment should be added to the respective repository or register.

A stakeholder review of the gap-analysis and resultant requirements architecture(s) should be held at the end of this phase.

Objectives, inputs and outputs

The inputs (▶,▲) and outputs (◀) are:

- identify and describe the gaps between the current 'as-is' context and proposed 'to-be' contexts of the iteration scope;
- identify and document requirements to resolve these gaps;
- partition these requirements to identify potential projects and/or programmes of work to implement the required changes.

The inputs and outputs are:

▲ Statement of Architecture Work (p.174)

▲ Architecture repository, including models for models for current and/or future architecture(s) (p.179)

▲ Requirements repository (p.180)

▲ Glossary and thesaurus (p.182)

▲ Issues / risks registers (p.180)

▶ Architecture-dispensations register (p.181)

◀ Phase-completion report – stakeholder review of gap-analysis (p.177)

Steps

As in Phase C, all steps other than the last – i.e. DX, the final stakeholder review – should be repeated for each time-horizon in scope. The stakeholder-review should cover and compare the 'as-is' architecture from Phase B to all 'to-be' architectures developed in Phase C.

Step D1 – Construct and validate matrix of 'as-is' to 'to-be' architectures

Draw up a matrix with all Architecture Building Blocks (ABBs) derived in Step B5 for the 'as-is' architecture on the vertical axis, and all ABBs derived in Step C5 for the respective 'to-be' architecture on the horizontal axis.

> Note that we do the gap-analysis with ABBs – *not* SBBs. The latter are pre-packaged suggestions for solutions – which we should *not* be looking at until we've derived the architectural requirements here, and the business-requirements for the solution (if any) in Phase E. It's worthwhile noting the upward links between ABBs and SBBs here, though, as they may hint at other ABBs we'll need for the gap-analysis.
>
> This is essentially the same gap-analysis technique as in TOGAF. It's a bit clunky, so if you already have a better technique, do use it instead. Otherwise It's probably simplest to stick with this one – it works well enough, and it's what most people already know.
>
> Another reason for using this technique is that if your architecture toolset supports TOGAF, it's likely that this matrix already exists as a standard report, drawn directly from the architecture repository – strongly recommended, if you can do it that way. If not, it's easy enough to set up in a spreadsheet or suchlike, anyway.

In creating the matrix it's essential to be consistent and accurate in use of terminology: use the glossary and thesaurus to identify where different names have been applied to the same or similar items, or items with similar names that are actually different.

Add to the 'as-is' axis a final row labelled 'New Items', and to the 'to-be' axis a final column labelled 'Eliminated Items'.

> Note too that 'New' and 'Eliminated' here are relative to the specific future-context – not to the architecture itself! We may well apply or re-use an 'eliminated' item elsewhere in the architecture, for example.

Where an ABB applies to both 'as-is' and 'to-be', record this with 'Retained' at the intersecting cell.

Review every case where an 'as-is' ABB seems to be missing in the future 'to-be' architecture:

- if the current item was correctly eliminated, mark it as such in the appropriate 'Eliminated Items' cell;
- if the current item is to be replaced, wholly or partly, by one or more items in the 'to-be', make a note to this effect in the corresponding intersecting cell(s);
- if the current item was unintentionally eliminated in the 'to-be', note this in the appropriate 'Eliminated' cell – the omission will need to be addressed in an iteration of the 'to-be' solution-design.

Where a 'to-be' ABB can't be found in the 'as-is' architecture, mark it at the intersection with the 'New Items' row, as a gap that needs to be filled, either by developing or procuring the entity(ies) implied by the new ABB.

When the assessment is complete, anything under 'Eliminated Items' or 'New Items' is a gap, which should either be explained as correctly eliminated, or marked as to be addressed either by re-instating or by developing or procuring the required item.

Step D2 – Derive change-requirements from validated matrix

From the gap-analysis matrix, use the links to ABBs to identify the underlying requirements represented by each item. New and/or eliminated items indicate requirements for change, whilst requirements from unchanged ABBs may also be relevant to solution designs.

By comparison between the 'as-is' and 'to-be' architectures, identify other primitives and composites which represent requirements or constraints on solution-designs for the architecture context.

Document these requirements and constraints in the context-specific section of the requirements-repository.

Step D3 – Review requirements against existing dispensations

Search the Dispensations register for existing dispensations that cover or intersect with the context of the iteration. Use the 'to-be' architecture to review relevant dispensations, to identify potential change-requirements to resolve those dispensations. This particularly applies to pseudo-ABBs, solution-designs masquerading as ABBs – see 'Solution Building Blocks (SBBs)' in Step B5 in *Methodology – assessment*, p. 135.

Document these requirements in the context-specific section of the requirements-repository.

Step D4 – Review requirements against qualitative criteria

Review the requirements derived in the previous step against the qualitative criteria selected in Step B4 of Phase B and for the respective time-horizon in Step C4 of Phase C. Where appropriate, amend the requirements to align with these criteria.

Step DX – Conduct checkpoint-review for stakeholders

Identify the stakeholders for the scope, as described in Steps BX and CX.

Collate the results of the previous steps, for *each* time-horizon in scope, and present these to the stakeholders for formal review under the governance procedures.

Merge the approved change-requirements into the requirements-repository, in accordance with requirements repository governance procedures.

If you've created additional architecture-models or views during this Phase, merge these as appropriate back into the segments of the architecture repository, in accordance with architecture-repository governance procedures.

Document the results of the review in a phase-completion-report. As advised by the stakeholders, you might also amend the *Statement of Architecture Work* to carry forward additional content and/or issues for subsequent phases of the iteration – for example, suggested solutions (Phase E), suggested project-structures (Phase F), potential architectural issues during implementation (Phase G), or notes for future architectural reviews (Phase H).

Application

- What methodology do you use at present for architectural assessment?
- What constraints – if any – does it place upon scope?
- If necessary, what would you need to change for it to be able to cover a full enterprise-wide scope?
- How does architectural assessment link in with governance for project- and programme-management?
- How do you engage your stakeholders in the architecture?
- In what ways could you improve stakeholder engagement in the architecture?
- What systems and processes do you have available to you to manage recording, maintenance and sharing of requirements,

issues, risks and opportunities, and architectural dispensations?

- What limitations are currently imposed on scope for such engagement and sharing? – for example, are requirements, issues and risks restricted solely to an IT scope, or even to an IT-architecture scope? By what means could you expand this to cover a full enterprise-wide scope? What issues would need to be resolved to do so?

Resources

TOGAF assessment phases: see www.opengroup.org/architecture/togaf8-doc/arch/toc.html (chapters from 'Phase A: Architecture Vision' to 'Phase D: Technology Architecture')

Viable Services modelling: see Tom Graves, 'The Viable Services Model: service quality, service interdependence and service completeness', in Jan van Bon [ed.], *IT Service Management: global best practices* (Van Haren, 2008)

VPEC-T: see www.lithandbook.com

VPEC-T: see Nigel Green, Carl Bate, *Lost In Translation: a handbook for information systems in the 21st century* (Evolved Technologist Press, 2007)

SqEME process modelling: see www.sqeme.nl/english/default.php

SqEME: see Jos van Oosten [ed.], *Process Management based on SqEME: SqEME Edition 2008*, (Van Haren, 2008)

Causal Layered Analysis: see www.metafuture.org/Articles/CausalLayeredAnalysis.htm

Causal Layered Analysis: see Sohail Inayatullah [ed.], *The Causal Layered Analysis (CLA) Reader: theory and case studies of an integrative and transformative methodology* (Taipei: Tamkang University Press, 2004)

Enterprise effectiveness modelling: see Tom Graves, *SEMPER and SCORE: enhancing enterprise effectiveness*, (Tetradian, 2008)

Whole-of-enterprise architecture: see Tom Graves, *Real Enterprise Architecture: beyond IT to the whole enterprise*, (Tetradian, 2008)

METHODOLOGY – SOLUTIONS

Summary

The second half of the architecture-cycle is focussed on detail-level design, implementation and deployment, and, at the end, lessons-learned from the iteration. Although domain-architects may be intensely involved in many of these processes, the enterprise-level architects should pull back to more of a support-role, maintaining a proactive 'watching brief' for any enterprise-wide architectural concerns.

Details

> Note that in some cases *there may be no solution-design required* once we've completed the assessment-phases. Sometimes we'll have already done all of the needed work in the assessment itself; sometimes it'll be more about attitude-shifts and the like, which will depend more on word-of-mouth and other narrative-techniques, and which don't need the whole formal project- or programme-management structure to bring them to fruition. Sometimes we'll start the solutions-phases, but stop part-way through, at Phase F or G, for example, because the work's already been done elsewhere. Either way, don't assume, in classic IT-centric style, that a 'solution' will always be needed – and especially, don't assume that everything needs an IT-based 'solution'!
>
> In fact, if at all possible, we should aim to avoid the need for conventional 'solutions', because they're invariably time-consuming and expensive. Far better to be a bit creative here, and find alternative approaches that will resolve the issues in a more agile and innovative way. We do the solutions-phases of the methodology only when we need them – not just as a matter of habit!

Solutions phases – an overview

In the solution phases – Phases E to H of the architecture-cycle – the emphasis shifts away from enterprise-level architecture, and more towards a background support for the detail needed to design, implement and deploy the changes implied by the requirements identified in the gap-analysis.

The focus of governance here moves to project- and programme-management, with enterprise architecture called upon mainly to provide architectural guidance and arbitration between projects, and to maintain high-level consistency as the architecture changes dynamically over time.

> If you're familiar with TOGAF, this too will be well-trodden ground –
> and is much the same as in the original ADM, too, because most of it
> isn't architecture's business anyway. Whilst the domain-architects
> would be busy, the main role for enterprise-architecture in these Phases
> is a watching-brief, providing architectural support and 'big-picture'
> overview, but otherwise keeping out of the way unless asked.
> Architecture is not design: and designers understandably do not like it
> when architects meddle in their work without good reason!
>
> As before, the main difference is one of scope: whilst TOGAF expects
> all solutions to be centred on IT, we shouldn't make any such
> assumption. In fact some, if not many, of the solutions here may
> involve no IT at all – which could well be a challenge at first if you've
> come from a conventional IT-centric background. But if you keep the
> focus on overall *effectiveness* – 'efficient *on purpose*' – you should be
> able to stay safely on track to support whatever's required.

The real complexity here is in the trade-offs between architectural 'purity' and real-world constraints. The most valuable skill of the enterprise-architect is the ability to find a balance between what is desirable and what is available and achievable, to derive solutions that are truly effective – efficient, reliable, elegant, appropriate, integrated – across the *whole* of the enterprise. Tact and diplomacy are essential character-traits here: consistency is important, but trying to enforce compliance via the 'architecture police' is *not* the way to do it...

For the same reasons, perhaps the greatest danger here is one of ego. Too often we've seen architects not only destroy their architecture, but damage their own careers and the credibility of architecture as a whole, in the hubris of trying to play 'the Creator of all' and suchlike. It's essential to remember that at the end, the architect is just one member of a much larger team tasked with creating change in the enterprise: it *is* important to stand up for our truth, but the ultimate authority here belongs to programme-governance, not to architecture.

Phase E – design solutions

During this phase you'll provide technical and other support to assist the sponsor in selecting appropriate options to resolve the gap between the 'as-is' and the one or more 'to-be' architectures for the context. Note that the key responsibility for decisions on solution designs rests with the sponsor, not the architecture unit.

Change-requirements, opportunities, risks and other issues, and architecture-models and lists of applicable ABBs and SBBs for the respective scope and context(s), are all key inputs to this process. Suggested solutions may also have been carried forward from previous Phases in the Statement of Architecture Work.

The primary output for the sponsor, and usually created by the sponsor, will be any number of high-level solution designs. (Note that in some cases, such as for some types of simple impact-analysis, a solution-design may not be required.) Your main responsibility here will be to ensure and affirm that such solution-designs are architecture-compliant.

Any requirements, issues and risks identified during the assessment will be added to the respective repository or register.

A stakeholder review of the solution-design(s) and architecture implications should be conducted at the end of this phase.

Objectives, inputs and outputs

The objectives of Phase E are to:

- assist the sponsor and change-management in evaluating and selecting among the implementation options identified by the requirements, and assessing implementation trade-offs (for example, build *versus* buy *versus* re-use options, and sub-options within those major options) ;
- assist the sponsor and change-management in identifying sequences of overall work-packages or projects to be undertaken in moving from 'as-is' to 'to-be'.

The inputs (►,▲) and outputs (◄) are:

▲ Statement of Architecture Work (p.174)

► Literature-review

► Product-literature, white-papers, research-studies and other material relevant to potential solution-designs for the context.

► Architecture-models repository and architecture models (p.179)

▲ Requirements repository (p.180)

▲ Glossary and thesaurus (p.182)

▲ Issues / risks registers (p.180)

▲ Architecture-dispensations register (p.181)

◄ Solution Design Document(s) (p.175)

◄ Phase-completion report – stakeholder review of solution design (p.177) (may be included or referenced in a stakeholder review of the broader project)

Steps

Typical steps include the following:

Step E1 – Review gap-analysis and requirements from Phase D

Reframe the requirements from Phase D into business rather than architectural terms, to describe the business requirements for solutions to the gaps identified for the context.

Merge any amended requirements into the requirements repository, creating '‹implements›' linkages to higher-order requirements as appropriate.

Step E2 – Identify business drivers and constraints for implementation

Identify any additional requirements for the context arising from higher-order business-principles and standards, from strategic and tactical business drivers and from operational, technical and other constraints.

Examples of business drivers include:

- reduction of costs
- consolidation of services
- introduction of new customer services, etc.

Examples of constraints include:

- operational restrictions required by new legislation
- minimum-system specification required to support a preferred solution
- sunset of vendor support for existing technology

As in the previous step, merge any new or amended requirements into the requirements-repository, creating '‹implements›' linkages to higher-order requirements as appropriate.

Step E3 – Derive technical requirements from functional perspective

Move the framework focus steadily downward, from higher-level architecture toward lower-level implementation designs. Use the scope of the architecture-cycle to point to relevant Solution Building Blocks (SBBs) and their component Architectural Building Blocks (ABBs), to identify further functional and/or qualitative requirements for solution designs. Note any conflicts between requirements and constraints, especially those already identified in the dispensations register.

As above, merge any new or amended requirements into the requirements repository, creating '‹implements›' or '‹conflicts with›' cross-references as appropriate.

Step E4 – Derive co-existence and interoperability requirements

Assess the edges of the architecture context for additional requirements needed to manage co-existence and interoperability with other systems. Examples include:

- *inter-agency protocol* – activities and information needed to transfer responsibility to or from a value-chain partner
- *process start- and end-events* – message-content and the like to trigger a business-process or to record its completion
- *shared interface* – protocol and messaging-format for a low-level inter-system interface such as an XML-based Enterprise Service Bus

Merge any new or amended requirements into the requirements repository, creating '‹implements›' or '‹conflicts with›' cross-references as appropriate.

Step E5 – Perform architecture re-assessment and gap analysis

Re-assess the architecture in relation to the requirements, constraints and conflicts identified in the previous steps. Note that it may be necessary to return to Phase C, or even to Phase B, if conflicts are severe enough to compel a more detailed architectural review.

Do a gap analysis – see 'Phase D – derive change-requirements' in *Methodology – assessment*, p. 140 – to attempt to resolve any constraints which conflict with the architecture. (In practice, there will almost always be *some* constraint-conflicts, especially at the operational level.) If any such conflicts cannot be resolved, document the constraints and architectural issues with one or more preliminary Architecture Dispensation records.

Step E6 – Develop preliminary solution designs

Assist the sponsor in developing proposals for a solution or set of solutions which would satisfy those requirements and constraints, in accordance with the architecture and any applicable architecture dispensations. A review of relevant product-literature, white-papers, research-studies and other material is also likely to be helpful in this.

Document these preliminary solution-designs as per the respective governance procedures.

Step E7 – Identify major work packages or projects

Assist the sponsor in describing an overall programme of work to implement the required solutions, by clustering the requirements into related work-packages or projects.

In general, aim to categorise these programme elements in terms of new development, purchase opportunity, or re-use of existing system – the classic 'build, buy or re-use'.

Document this proposed programme of work as per the respective change-management governance procedures.

Step EX – Conduct stakeholder review of solution designs

Collate the results of the previous steps, for *each* time-horizon in scope, and assist the sponsor in presenting these to the stake-holders for formal review under the governance procedures.

Document the results of the review in a phase-completion-report. As before, you may need to amend the *Statement of Architecture Work* to carry forward additional content and/or issues for subsequent phases of the architecture cycle – for example, suggested project structures (Phase F), potential architectural issues during implementation (Phase G), or notes for future architectural reviews (Phase H).

Phase F – plan implementation

During Phase F – applicable only if one or more solution-designs were developed in Phase E – the architecture unit provides technical and other support to assist the sponsor, in conjunction with the respective programme-management body, in developing project- or migration-plans to implement the proposed solution designs. The key responsibility for such decisions rests with the sponsor and programme management body, not the architecture unit.

Issues, risks, change-requirements, and architecture-models and lists of applicable ABBs and SBBs for the respective scope and context(s), are all key inputs to this process.

The primary output for the sponsor, and usually created together by the sponsor and change-management, will be any number of project- and/or migration-plans. (Note that for some solution-designs, a project- or migration-plan may not be required.) The responsibility of the architecture unit here will be to assess and affirm that such plans are architecture-compliant, and also to advise on any inter-project conflicts or opportunities for shared facilities and other synergies.

Any requirements, issues and risks identified during the assessment will be added to the respective repository or register.

A stakeholder review of the plan(s) and architecture implications should be conducted at the end of this phase.

Objectives, inputs and outputs

The objectives of Phase F are to:

- sort the solution designs into priority order
- develop project- and/or migration-plans to implement the proposed solution-designs
- assess the dependencies, costs, and benefits of the various projects
- sort the implementation plans into delivery order
- generate an overall implementation and migration strategy and a detailed Implementation Plan

The inputs (▶,▲) and outputs (◀) are:

- ▲ Statement of Architecture Work (p.174)
- ▶ Solution Design Document (p.175)
- ▲ Architecture Compliance Statement (p.175)
- ▶ Architecture-models repository (p.179)
- ▲ Requirements repository (p.180)
- ▲ Glossary and thesaurus (p.182)
- ▲ Issues / risks registers (p.180)
- ▲ Architecture-dispensations register (p.181)
- ◀ Project-plan(s) or Migration-plan(s) (p.175)
- ◀ Phase-completion report – stakeholder review of migration-plan (p.177)

Steps

The steps to be covered during this phase depend on programme governance rather than architecture governance. In developing a migration and implementation plan for IT systems, one common approach is to implement business functions in a data-driven chronological sequence: create the applications and supporting technology that create data before those that process the data, before those that simply store, archive, or delete data. For manual or machine-based processes, the equivalent strategy would be to start with processes that emphasise service-delivery, and move on from there to implement the processes that monitor and manage service-delivery – though there's a danger that the latter might be omitted under pressure of work. From a business perspective, though, the most successful basic strategy for architecture is to focus initially on projects that will deliver short-term pay-offs and so create an impetus for proceeding with longer-term projects.

Much of the architectural detail here will be handled by domain-architects and solution-designers – as described, for example, in the equivalent of this Phase in the TOGAF ADM specification. The main role for enterprise-architecture here is to assist in maintaining a high-level view and in identifying the trade-offs between projects, and trade-offs and interdependencies over time, within the time-scale of the overall scope of the architecture iteration.

In practice, enterprise-architecture in Phase F has more of a watching-brief than an active role, so the key steps here would depend on broader governance procedures for detail-level project management, programme management and change management. The TOGAF ADM, for example, suggests that typical programme-management steps would include:

Step F1 – Prioritise projects

Step F2 – Estimate resource requirements and availability

Step F3 – Perform cost/benefit assessment of the various migration projects

Step F4 – Perform risk assessment

Step F5 – Generate timelined implementation roadmap

Step F6 – Document the Migration Plan

Step FX – Conduct stakeholder review of project- or migration-plan

Prior to the final review of the respective project- or migration-plan, collate the results of architectural engagement in each of the previous steps, and present these to the architecture stakeholders for formal review under the governance procedures.

Document the results of the review in a phase-completion-report. As advised by the stakeholders, you may again need to amend the *Statement of Architecture Work* to carry forward additional content and/or issues for subsequent phases of the architecture cycle – for example, potential architectural issues during implementation (Phase G), or notes for future architectural reviews (Phase H).

Phase G – guide implementation

During this phase – applicable only if one or more project- or migration-plans were developed in Phase F – the architecture unit provides technical and other support to assist the sponsor, in conjunction with the respective programme-management body, to attain and maintain architecture-compliance during implementation of the selected solution from Phase E, in accordance with the project- or migration-plan from Phase F. Overall governance for the project(s) under review remains with the respective project- or programme-management body.

> Note that the detail of what happens in this Phase depends on the governance model used by the PMO or its equivalent. The description here is based on what we did in business-transformation for a large logistics enterprise, but it might be different in your own context. Ask the PMO what they use, and negotiate a suitable set of tactics.
>
> I've also assumed that, as in the PRINCE2-based model we used in that case, there would be multiple governance-'gateways' in the project lifecycle, with a go/no-go review at each. Architectural input would be involved at each of these gateways, particularly around compliance and cross-project integration. Projects take *time* to progress: we revisit architectural compliance of proposals at each gateway in part because the architecture may have moved on in the intervening time.
>
> Do remember, though, that your aim is to help things happen in the enterprise, not just to enforce architectural 'purity': beware of the risk of coming over as the heavy-handed 'architecture police', because that's a really quick way to make enemies and lose influence with people!

Once again, the enterprise-architecture unit here will typically maintain a watching-brief rather than take an active role. The primary input and output for the sponsor, and created by the sponsor, will be one or more *Architecture Compliance Statement* documents. Dependent on programme-management governance, one *Architecture Compliance Statement* will usually be required at each key gateway in the solution-implementation process. The architecture responsibility here will be to confirm that the project-summaries in each *Compliance Statement* are indeed architecture-compliant, and to document any variances and recommended resolutions for non-conformances in either an *Architecture Position Statement* or, for necessarily-non-compliant solutions, an *Architecture Dispensation Statement*.

Any requirements, issues and risks identified during the assessment will be added to the respective repository or register.

A stakeholder review of the plan(s) and the architecture compliance, position and dispensation statements and their architecture implications should be conducted at the end of this phase.

Objectives, inputs and outputs

The objectives of Phase G are to:

- maintain architecture governance whilst solutions are designed, implemented and deployed
- ensure conformance with the defined architecture by implementation projects and other projects
- formulate architecture recommendations for implementation projects
- assist programme- and project-managers in identifying architecture-compliant opportunities for inter-project synergies that may arise during design and implementation

The inputs (►, ▲) and outputs (◄) are:

- ▲ Statement of Architecture Work (p.174)
- ► Project-plan or Migration-plan (p.175)
- ▲ Architecture Compliance Statement (p.175)
- ► Architecture-models repository (p.179)
- ▲ Requirements repository (p.180)
- ▲ Glossary and thesaurus (p.182)
- ▲ Issues / risks registers (p.180)
- ▲ Architecture-dispensations register (p.181)
- ◄ Architecture Position Statement (p.176)
- ◄ Architecture Dispensation Statement (p.177)
- ◄ Phase-completion report – stakeholder review of implementation (p.177)

Steps

The precise steps taken in Phase G will depend on the requirements and the number of gateways in the respective governance methodology. All steps other than the last – i.e. GX, the final stakeholder-review, at project-completion – should be repeated for each governance gateway. The final review should assess architectural issues arising during all gateways for the implementation plan in scope for the architecture-cycle.

From the architecture perspective, engagement at each gateway – typically, Conceptual Design, Detailed Solution Design, draft Request For Quote or Request For Tender, etc – begins with the receipt of the *Architecture Compliance Statement* for the respective project-governance stage.

Key steps at each gateway will typically include:

Step G1 – Review Architecture Compliance Statement

At each gateway, and for each implementation project, subject to governance rules, the sponsor or project-manager should fill in and deliver an Architecture Compliance Statement. This should indicate the specific scope of the project, and specify the degree to which the plan or design for the project stage complies with the architecture for the respective time-horizon, identifying any non-conformances.

Assess any non-conformances listed, especially those which are not already covered by an Architecture Dispensation Statement.

Document any issues identified, for broader-scope review in the next step.

Step G2 – Assess impact on overall architecture

Using the scope specified in the Architecture Compliance Statement, assess the probable impact on the overall architecture for the respective time-horizon. Sources of impact would include not only non-conformances and dispensations, but also opportunities implied by what or how the project intends to deliver its solution. For example:

- *duplicate functionality*: two or more projects creating the same functionality – sometimes in the same nominal space
- *incompatible functionality*: two or more projects using different and incompatible technologies to deliver the same business-functions – again, sometimes even in the same physical space
- *opportunity for synergy*: minor changes to one or more projects that would deliver additional synergies – i.e. greater *overall* business-effectiveness
- *opportunity for schedule-improvement*: a project delivers a technology or capability earlier in the schedule expected by one or more other projects

Document any identified issues, risks or opportunities in the respective registers, and notify project stakeholders as appropriate.

Step G3 – Respond to Architecture Compliance Statement

Where assessment indicates that a response is required, summarise any architectural issues identified in the previous steps, and return this to the sponsor or project-manager in the form of an Architecture Position Statement and/or Architecture Dispensation Statement.

Provide assistance to the project as appropriate to resolve these issues where practicable.

Step GX – Conduct stakeholder architectural review of plan-implementation

Collate the results of the previous steps from all gateways, and present these to the stakeholders for formal review under the governance procedures.

Document the results of the review in a phase-completion-report. As advised by the stakeholders, you may need to amend the *Statement of Architecture Work* to carry forward additional content and/or issues for the last phase of the architecture iteration, the end-of-cycle architectural review (Phase H).

Phase H – review lessons-learned

During this phase the architecture unit will review the results of the iteration in terms benefits achieved to the business, and of the implications and impact on the overall future architecture. This will often result in updates or additions to the set of primitives, models, metamodels, Architectural Building Blocks, Solution Building Blocks and other content in the Enterprise Continuum; to requirements, standards and other decisions in the requirements-repository; to content within the shared glossary and thesaurus; and/or to entries in the issues-register and risks-register. A stakeholder review of the overall architecture cycle will be conducted at the end of this phase.

> In the conventional 'big-bang' approach to architecture, this is a distinct phase within each architecture cycle, because there's only one architecture cycle happening at any given time. But in the full iterative approach described here, there may well be dozens of different cycles happening at once, all at different speeds, with some Phase G implementations taking perhaps as little as a couple of days and others maybe as much as a couple of years. Under those conditions, a separate Phase H for each cycle starts to make less sense.
>
> So as the architecture maturity develops, and the number of cycles increases, you'll probably start to run Phase H not as a distinct cycle-related phase, but as a regular review meeting, perhaps once a month, or even once a week, adjusting the scope to assess whatever's been completed during that period. But whilst the governance needs to change a bit to suit, the review-steps themselves are essentially the same either way – keep it simple, as usual.

One or more new *Request for Architecture Work* documents, for further assessment within new architecture cycles, may be raised as a result of this review. Any out-of-scope requirements, issues and risks identified during the assessment will be added to the respective repository or register, for action by the appropriate body.

Objectives, inputs and outputs

The objectives of Phase H are to:

- identify changes to architecture indicated by completion of the cycle
- initiate work to implement those changes, including any needed analysis

The inputs (▶,▲) and outputs (◀) are:

▲ Statement of Architecture Work (p.174)

▲ Architecture-models repository (p.179)

▲ Requirements repository (p.180)

▲ Glossary and thesaurus (p.182)

▲ Issues / risks registers (p.180)

▲ Architecture-dispensations register (p.181)

▶ Project- and programme-development documentation, including project-plans (p.175), Architecture Compliance Statements (p.175), etc

◀ Request(s) for Architecture Work (p.172)

Steps

Key steps in Phase H include:

Step H1 – Assess results from the architecture-cycle

Review all materials developed or changed during the architecture cycle, including:

- Request for Architecture Work
- Statement of Architecture Work
- Architecture-models – also models created in project-development
- Architecture and Solution Building Blocks and their 'bindedness'
- Requirements, in repository and in project-specific documents
- Issues in issues-register
- Opportunities and risks in risks-register
- Architecture Compliance Statements
- Architecture Position Statements
- Architecture Dispensations, and Dispensations register

Follow up and resolve any actions required by entries in the issues-register for this architecture-cycle, in architecture Position or Dispensation statements, and in other governance-documents.

Summarise any requirements for change in the architecture that may occur as a result of this assessment.

Note that all issues listed in the issues-register that relate to the current architecture-cycle *must* be resolved before this phase can be signed off as complete.

Assess what other architectural changes, if any, are implied or suggested by the items listed above.

Document the results of the assessment in a temporary register created for this phase.

Step H2 – Monitor changes in the business environment

Use the end-of-cycle assessment as an opportunity to review applicable enterprise strategies and upcoming changes in the business environment, in technology, in legislation, etc, and their possible impacts on the enterprise architecture. Common strategy-assessment tools such as scenarios, environmental scanning and business intelligence will be helpful in this, and should be viewed as a standard part of the architecture-development toolkit.

Note any implied opportunities or risks, and assess any potential for changes to the architecture, including scope for new Architecture Building Blocks and Solution Building Blocks.

Document architectural issues or risks in the temporary register; document other issues or risks in the appropriate issues or risks registers.

Step H3 – Assess potential changes to framework, methodology etc

Conduct a brief lessons-learned exercise to review the overall architecture process, including:

- framework
- methodology
- governance
- principles
- standards
- glossary and thesaurus

Document any suggested additions, amendments or other changes in the temporary register.

Step H4 – Assess requirements and options for architecture change

Review the content of the temporary register to assess requirements and options for architecture change.

Document proposals for change and/or further analysis in one or more *Request For Architecture Work* documents.

Step HX – Conduct review by architecture governance-body

Collate the results of the previous steps, and present the proposals and their related background to the architecture-governance body for formal review. The aim of the review is to agree on actions to be taken to update the architecture in response to the lessons-learned from the present architecture-cycle.

On completion, merge into the appropriate permanent register for risks, issues or dispensations any content from the amended temporary register which needs to be retained.

The *Statement of Architecture Work* may be amended to summarise the overall results of the architecture-cycle, as a completion-report both for this phase and for the architecture-cycle as a whole.

Application

- What role does enterprise architecture take at present in solution design, implementation and deployment?
- What governance roles, rules and methodologies currently apply to architectural involvement in solution-development?
- What mechanisms do you have in place at present to manage dynamic changes to architecture over time, as a result of new technologies, new practices, new partners and the like? How do you manage the resultant interactions and trade-offs between architecture and solution-development?
- What 'lessons learned' processes do you currently follow to review the architecture itself at the end of a sequence of architectural activities?
- In what ways would – or should – these roles, responsibilities and methodologies change as you expand the architecture outward to a full enterprise-wide scope?

Resources

🕸 TOGAF solution phases: see www.opengroup.org/architecture/togaf8-doc/arch/toc.html (chapters from 'Phase E: Opportunities and Solutions' to 'Phase H: Architecture Change Management')

METHODOLOGY – HANDS-OFF ARCHITECTURE

Summary

In complex contexts with high rates of change, a more mature enterprise architecture capability can take a hands-off approach, allowing some aspects of the architecture to emerge naturally from the complexity. Note, though, that use of such a strategy in an inappropriate context or with immature architecture could result in chaos, with expensive results all round: it should only be attempted when the risks and trade-offs are fully understood and addressed.

Details

Hands-off architecture – an overview

The main reasons for using a 'hands-off' architecture are to support agility, innovation and reinforcement of responsibility in the overall enterprise. When done properly, it also permits significant reductions in the direct workload and size of the architecture team. The effective staff-cost savings may not seem all that much, as the expertise moves from the core team more into the project space; but the overall cost-savings and other benefits from a distributed architecture should continue to increase steadily as architectural awareness becomes more of a habit throughout the enterprise.

In hands-off architecture, the architectural work revolves around an expanded equivalent of Phase G in the main methodology. In effect, collective responsibility for architecture assessment – the equivalent of Phases A to D in the main methodology – is passed to the project-sponsors, extending their existing responsibilities for the Phase E to H solution-stages. The architecture team maintains a watching-brief over all projects and programmes that pass through the Programme Management Office, intervening with advice, suggestions and requests for change only where appropriate, and in line with the overall aims for the architecture.

There is no predefined plan or 'blueprint' for the architecture. Instead, the effective architecture is allowed to emerge organically in relation to a set of specific and clearly-enunciated architectural principles, emphasising overall *effectiveness* for each project in relation to the whole.

The overall process resembles that for a building project in a city-planning context, and has two distinct phases or gateways – the 'notify gateway', and the 'as-built gateway'.

At the first gateway, the sponsor presents to the 'planning authority' – typically the Programme Management Office – a description of how the project will satisfy any mandatory requirements ('building regulations') and the architectural principles ('planning approval'). Much as with a city-planning exercise, the description would be published, to allow other sponsors and stakeholders to comment and collaborate on amending their own projects, and also to permit the architecture team to intervene as appropriate. Where concerns or disputes arise, the PMO would act as a tribunal, with the architecture team in the role of expert advisor, to arrive at a negotiated agreement on changes to the project.

The sponsor then implements the project, and on completion – the as-built gateway – presents another description that summarises what was actually done over the intervening period, to allow the architecture team to again review the impact and 'lessons learned' for the overall architecture of the collective enterprise. This then feeds back into the architecture principles and guidelines for subsequent projects.

Preparation

Hands-off-architecture depends on a clear set of principles, and one or more Reference Frameworks to provide explicit articulation of the lists of items which are mandatory, desirable, recommended and the like – the enterprise equivalent of building-regulations and city-development policy.

The architecture principles should be developed and authorised in an equivalent of the 'Phase P' preliminaries in the main methodology – see *Methodology – preparation*, p.113.

The Reference Frameworks should be developed over a number of architecture iterations, preferably including assessment phases – see *Methodology – assessment*, p.121 – and implementation reviews – see *Methodology – solutions*, p.146.

Appropriate governance procedures will also need to be in place, and likewise some means to publish and comment on the change-

162

proposals, and to manage the resultant requirements, issues, risks, dispensations and the like.

> You'll also need a significant amount of architecture maturity before this will work – not just the reference-frameworks, but overall engagement of people throughout the enterprise in the architectural process. In short, don't even *think* of doing hands-off architecture unless all of these things are in place and in daily use – because without them you'll get nowhere, badly.
>
> We've seen a few examples already where people have tried to do so too early – in one instance solely as a cost-cutting exercise, which is rarely a good idea – and the results have invariably been messy, painful and expensive. Test the waters with a small, local experiment, perhaps, but don't try it on a full enterprise-wide scale unless you *know* you're ready: as the old adage puts it, don't try to run before you can walk – or crawl!

As with the 'Phase P' preliminaries, it would be advisable to re-assess and, where necessary, update the principles and reference-frameworks at regular intervals – certainly at least once each year – and publish any changes through the same mechanisms.

'Notify' gateway

The 'hands-off' process is one of management by exception, rather than by routine intervention and control as in the main methodology. The initial trigger for the process is the arrival of a project architectural description – see 'Architecture Description Statement' in *Completion – architecture artefacts*, p.176. This is provided by the project sponsor or project-manager, typically via the Programme Management Office, and describes how the project will conform to the mandatory rules, guidelines and principles published by the architecture team.

> In effect, this is a bundled report from the equivalent of Phases A to C of the main methodology – the purpose, 'as-is' and 'to-be' stages – except that the assessment will have been done by the project team rather than the architects, and the whole thing is packed inside what would otherwise have been Phase G, the implementation stage.
>
> The architecture team may well have provided some assistance to the project before all this happens, but the whole aim here is that the onus for getting it right should be more on the project team rather than the architecture unit – hence 'hands-off' architecture, after all.

The architecture team carries out a quick review of the description, to check that it does conform to the published requirements, and also to look for possible synergies with other projects – although ideally that should already have been done by the Programme Management Office.

If the team consider that action need be taken, a response document is prepared, describing the team's concerns – see 'Architecture Position Statement' in *Completion – architecture artefacts*, p.176. This is returned to the project sponsor – again, typically via the Programme Management Office – together with a request to carry out a joint review of the proposal from an architectural perspective. Sometimes the issue will be that a project's intentions clash with the architecture, but in some cases it may be that the project is introducing an innovation that could be valuable elsewhere in the enterprise, and the architecture team are asking the project's advice on how to do this – in other words, it needs to be seen as a two-way street, not solely an 'edict from above'.

The outcome of this review may include recommended changes to the project or to a group of projects; a formal dispensation – see 'Architecture Dispensation Statement' in *Completion – architecture artefacts*, p.177; or changes to the architecture itself, via the equivalent of the Phase H end-of-cycle review in the main methodology. This in turn may trigger new architecture cycles, and also updates to the published architecture principles and guidelines.

'As-built' gateway

A similar architecture description should be created at the end of the project implementation, as part of the project's own 'lessons learned' review. The aim here is simply to notify the architecture team of what was actually implemented and delivered – which may not be the same as in the original plan.

> No response-document would be needed here, of course, because the project is over and done with – the architecture team can't change that. But what we *can* do is update the architecture, and again let other projects know about any lessons learned from the exercise. It's all part of maintaining stakeholder engagement in the development of the architecture, as an *enterprise-wide* shared resource.

This is the direct equivalent of the Phase H review at the end of the main methodology's architecture cycle. As at the end of the 'notify' gateway, this may trigger new architecture cycles, or updates to the published architecture principles and guidelines.

Application

- What engagement do projects already have in your existing architecture?

- How much of your existing architecture – particularly principles, guidelines and reference-frameworks – is published and generally accessible throughout the enterprise?
- To what extent are projects and Programme Management Office ready and able to do their own architectural assessments? What could you do to extend that capability?
- To what extent are you ready to run a hands-off architecture? What would you need to do – what would need to change – to make it possible? What level of maturity would be needed in the existing architecture to make this happen?
- How would you describe and present to management the business-case for a hands-off architecture?

Resources

- Agile Manifesto: see agilemanifesto.org
- Agile Enterprise Architecture: see agileea.wikidot.com
- Martin van den Berg, Marlies van Steenbergen, *Building an Enterprise Architecture Practice: tools, tips, best practices, ready-to-use insights* (Sogeti / Springer Verlag, 2006)

COMPLETION – AN OVERVIEW

Summary

Architecture is a continuous process, and needs nurturing to grow into ever more useful forms. We do this through communication and feedback, through discussion and dialogue with our business community, and through measuring the value of what we do.

Details

If architecture was only about design and implementation, all of our work would complete at the end of each architecture cycle. But we need to take both a broader and more long-term view than that: architecture is not a once-off 'fit and forget', but an ongoing process, always reaching to enhance maturity and improve overall business value.

To do this, we need to *measure* maturity, using one of the proven architecture maturity-models, as described earlier – see 'Metrics products' in *Governance – products*, p.51. We also need to measure the business-value and benefits-realisation from the architecture work, for each individual change-project, and for the enterprise as a whole.

> Do beware, though, of the tendency to attempt to measure everything solely in monetary terms — particularly short-term 'return on investment'. The *real* anchors for success-metrics are the enterprise vision and values: for a commercial organisation, financial return does need to be in there somewhere, but not as the only one!

Architecture links everything together. It does not exist on its own – it's just one more capability within the enterprise – but it can certainly help to link the disparate parts of the enterprise together into a unified whole. This too is the role of enterprise-architecture: there are many domain-architectures, such as process architecture, or technology architecture for IT; there are 'vertical' architectures such as capability architecture and data architecture; there are 'pervasive' architectures such as security architecture and strategy architecture; but *enterprise* architecture links all these architectures together. That's our real business function *as* enterprise architects, and we need to confirm that we're doing it well.

As each architecture-cycle ends, we should already be setting up for the next: architecture is a continuous process, not a project. And as custodians of a specific body of knowledge – the enterprise's "knowledge of its purpose, its structure and itself", to return to that earlier definition – we need to ensure that it is extended, managed, maintained on behalf of the *whole* enterprise. Which means we *must* create and engage in a constant dialogue with and between architecture stakeholders. An increased awareness across the whole enterprise about architectural issues is perhaps *the* key outcome of architectural practice: so gathering feedback, and *using* it, is a key part of that process.

All those architectural artefacts we produce – documents, models, lists of requirements and risks and the like – will only be useful if people know about them and know how to use them. That's where dialogue comes into the picture; likewise some kind of built-in publishing facilities – typically web-based for intranet or extranet – in the enterprise-architecture toolset.

But first we need a better understanding of what all those artefacts *are* – their content, their audience, how and why they're used. The next section summarises the main types of artefact we're likely to produce in architecture work; after that we'll return to the wrap-up – how we complete each process in order to keep the architecture growing.

Application

- How do you identify that your enterprise architecture work has been successful? How do you and your clients define 'success' in that sense?
- What metrics do you use at present? What metrics could or should you use in future, as the scope of your work expands to the whole-of-enterprise level?
- How do you publish and promulgate the results of your work at present? What architecture artefacts do you produce?
- What mechanisms exist to garner and incorporate feedback into the architecture? What can you do to make that happen, and to verify the quality of what happens?
- What could you do to enhance awareness and engagement by the enterprise in its architecture?
- What 'lessons learned' processes do you apply at the end of each architecture cycle? What governance and other

mechanisms ensure that those lessons are applied in subsequent cycles?

Resources

📖 Martin van den Berg, Marlies van Steenbergen, *Building an Enterprise Architecture Practice: tools, tips, best practices, ready-to-use insights* (Sogeti / Springer Verlag, 2006)

📖 Meta Group Architecture Maturity Audit: *Meta Group Practice,* (2000), Vol 4 No.4 (for Part 1) and No.5 (for Part 2)

📖 Whole-of-enterprise architecture: see Tom Graves, *Real Enterprise Architecture: beyond IT to the whole enterprise,* (Tetradian, 2008)

COMPLETION – ARCHITECTURE ARTEFACTS

Summary

The most visible end-product of enterprise-architecture is the set of documents and other artefacts created during the various stages of the methodology and its governance. Most of these artefacts should be created, maintained and managed in a controlled, disciplined manner, to provide a stable reference for future use and reuse. This section describes the main types of artefacts or 'products', their contents, purpose and stakeholders.

Details

A key result of the architecture process is the creation of a wide range of architectural artefacts or 'products', to use the PRINCE2 term. Some of these are used for governance of architecture and the architecture-cycle (see *Governance – products*, p.48); others – such as risks- and issues-registers or the glossary and thesaurus – are used for shared reference; and others – particularly the requirements repository and the broad range of architecture-models – are used to guide solution-designs.

These artefacts also represent part of the performance of architecture. They're summarised here under two groupings: for governance, either overall or for a single architecture-cycle; and repositories, models and other shared artefacts which may be created, updated and re-used in successive architecture cycles.

The people who create, review and sign-off documents and other products are referenced here by their generic roles. Examples include:

- *architect*: person conducting enterprise-architecture work
- *architecture lead*: person responsible for overall conduct of enterprise-architecture work
- *architecture unit*: organisational grouping of people doing enterprise-architecture work
- *sponsor*: person requesting architecture-work, and authorised to allocate resources towards such work

- *project lead*: person responsible for execution of a solution-implementation plan, usually on behalf of the sponsor
- *governance body*: formal grouping to provide oversight of architecture, solution-design, project-/programme-management or other work
- *governance lead*: person responsible for overall conduct of a governance body
- *programme-management body*: organisational grouping of persons conducting programme- or project-management across a business domain or across the whole organisation
- *programme-management lead*: person responsible for overall conduct of a programme-management body
- *delegate*: person authorised to act and/or sign on behalf of the sponsor, architecture lead, governance lead, programme-management lead, etc

Governance products

Architecture Charter

The Architecture Charter identifies the authorised overall scope and guiding principles for subsequent architecture work. It describes the overall role and scope of the architecture from a business perspective, and the architecture team, and their roles, responsibilities and function within the organisation, and provides the formal authority to do the enterprise-architecture work.

It is created or reviewed by the architecture lead or delegate during the Preliminary Phase, and signed-off by the sponsor of the architecture work – usually executive level – and/or by the governance lead for architecture. It is referenced during all Phases by architects; potential requestors for architecture services, governance bodies, and other stakeholders.

Typical content should include:
- summary of the results of the Preliminary Phase:
- core definitions of architecture, role of architecture within the organisation, governance, frameworks, methodologies, etc
- organisational and operational scope of architecture
- performance criteria – key performance indicators, critical success factors, service levels, etc
- includes all methodology and governance documents by reference

170

- formal authority to conduct architecture development and provide architecture services to other business units

Architecture Governance

The Architecture Governance document specifies the governance procedures to be followed in architecture work. It identifies the processes, roles and responsibilities for architecture governance.

Creation and usage are the same as for the Architecture Charter.

Typical content should include:

- description of overall governance context, including identification of higher-level governance (included by reference)
- membership, roles and responsibilities of governance bodies for different types of architecture work
- procedures for governance of different types of architecture work
- procedures for escalation in case of conflicts or higher-level issues
- procedures for management of architectural-modelling and architecture-information repository
- procedures for management of requirements and requirements-repository
- procedures for management of issues and issues-register (including opportunities etc)
- procedures for management of risks and risks-register
- procedures for management of architectural-dispensations and dispensations-register

Architecture Principles

The Architecture Principles specify the highest level of the reference architecture for the enterprise, and comprise one or more documents to identify and describe the core principles that will apply to all architecture.

It is created or reviewed by the architecture team and the governance body during the Preliminary Phase, and signed-off by the architecture sponsor and the governance lead. It is referenced during all Phases by architects; potential requestors for architecture services, governance bodies, and other stakeholders.

Typical content should include:

- formal definition of architecture principles – may be split into sub-categories, for example:
  - overall principles
  - business-architecture principles
  - information principles
  - data principles
  - application principles
  - security principles
  - technology/infrastructure principles, etc
- includes organisation-wide principles by reference

Architecture Standards

The Architecture Standards ensure consistency of architecture description, and comprise one or more documents to identify and describe the standards to be used in developing architecture-models, requirements-models, etc.

Creation and usage are the same as for the Architecture Principles.

Typical content should include:

- formal specifications for applicable methodologies and frameworks
- formal standards for all architecture-model types
- formal standards for requirement-model types
- specifications of tools and techniques to be used for architecture development, etc
- other formal standards as required
- includes government, industry, international and other external standards by reference.

Request for Architecture Work

The Request authorises an item of architecture work: either the overall development of the architecture capability, in the Preliminary Phase, or an architecture-cycle starting at Phase A. The same document, or document structure, is used both types of architecture work.

It is created and signed off by the sponsor: for a Preliminary Phase, usually a senior executive such as the CEO, CFO, CIO or COO; or for regular architecture iterations starting at Phase A, any requestor within the enterprise. It is referenced in all respective

Phases by architects and by the governance bodies and stake-holders for the work.

Typical content should include:

- sponsor(s) authorising the work (including cost-code, if required)
- end-customer(s) for the work (if different from sponsor)
- purpose of the work (may be anything from a quick impact-analysis to a project architecture-compliance assessment to a full strategic-architecture review)
- scope of the work:
  - business-units involved (and their respective organisations, in a multi-partner context)
  - framework scope in broad terms, i.e. high-level strategy versus low-level execution, and assets versus functions versus requirements, etc
  - architecture-category scope, for example:
    - business-architecture
    - process-architecture
    - information-architecture
    - data-architecture
    - application-architecture
    - technology/infrastructure-architecture
    - security-architecture, etc
- schedule of the work (as indicated by purpose and scope: may be anything from a few hours to several weeks or months)
  - this may also need to align with authorised work-cycles in other projects or programmes
- context of the work (business-context, sufficient to identify the regions of architecture required, and appropriate views, viewpoints and model-types); may include, for example:
  - for an impact-analysis:
    - issues or components to be assessed
    - depth of assessment required (e.g. low-level execution impact only, linkage to strategic imperatives, etc)
    - breadth of assessment required (e.g. within a specific business-unit, across whole division, etc)
  - for a full architectural review:
    - overall vision and values
    - business goals (and changes)

- strategic plans and objectives
- time limits
- changes in the business environment (e.g. legislation, merger/demerger, etc)
- organisational constraints, including budgetary or financial constraints and other external constraints
- current business-system description
- current applicable IT and/or other execution-level structures and constraints
- description of resources available to developing organisation

Note that whilst this may be related to a business-case, this document typically should not include business-case concerns such as financials or business-benefits. In effect, a Request for Architecture Work may provide content for a business-case, or may arise as a follow-on outcome of a successful business-case, but would not in itself *be* the business-case.

Statement of Architecture Work

The Statement of Architecture Work acts as the specification of and continuing authority for work to be carried out, the record of governance for the work, and a container for the results of the work. It is also included by reference in the completion-reports for each phase.

It is created by the architect and sponsor during Phase A, updated by architects as required during subsequent Phases, and referenced by architects; requestors for architecture services; governance bodies and other stakeholders in Phases B to H.

Typical content should include:
- authority, contacts, time-frame for architecture work
- includes *Request for Architecture Work* by reference
- applicable principles, standards etc (included by reference)
- agreed business-purpose, business-scope and summary of work to be done in subsequent Phases
- work-breakdown and schedule (may be included by reference)
- applicable governance (if any) in addition to architecture-governance (e.g. relationship to an existing project or broader programme of work)

- architectural scope and context, analysis-methods, architectural views and viewpoints etc (for Phase B and C)
- final and any intermediate time-horizons etc (for Phase C);
- known gaps etc (for Phase D);
- opportunities, risks and potential solutions etc (for Phase E);
- project- or migration-plan issues etc (for Phase F);
- implementation-governance issues etc (for Phase G);
- summary of out-of-scope opportunities and other issues (in *Issues register*) and risks (in *Risks register*) for future architectural iterations or reviews (for Phase H)

Solution Design Document

High-level Solution Design Documents are created by solution architects and others as appropriate during Phase E, and referenced by developers and other stakeholders in Phases F and G.

The content should usually be out of scope for enterprise architects.

Project-plan or Migration-plan

The detailed Project Plans or Migration Plans are created by programme managers and others as appropriate during Phase F, with input from architects. They are referenced by developers, architects and other stakeholders in Phase G.

The content should usually be out of scope for enterprise architects.

Architecture Compliance Statement

The Architecture Compliance Statement is created by the project lead or solution designer as a design input to the architecture compliance reviews in Phase G. It identifies the extent to which the respective solution is or is not architecture-compliant, and documents the context of any non-conformances. It may be amended by designers in response to the compliance-review. Collectively, compliance-statements document programme-wide architecture compliance.

It is referenced in Phase G by system designers, developers; architects; programme-management body; sponsor and other requestors for architecture services, the stakeholders or 'owners' of items in scope for the architectural cycle; governance bodies; and other stakeholders. It is also used as input to the end-of-cycle review in Phase II.

Typical content should include:

- identifiers for project, responsible persons and solution-implementation stage
- architecture-compliance checklist
- list of non-conformances (if any) and proposed means of resolution

The content may be amended during Phase G to include descriptions of actions taken to resolve identified non-conformances.

Architecture Description Statement

The Architecture Description Statement is the key document used in 'hands-off' architecture. It is prepared by project-managers and solution-designers, in a standardised format, to notify enterprise architects about decisions taken and design content for as-is, to-be and as-built business solutions. The purpose of the document is to aid architects in creating an overall picture of design and development activity in the enterprise, from which to garner suggestions about changes to promote or dissuade so as to enhance the overall effectiveness of the enterprise.

Typical content should include:

- identifiers for project, responsible persons and solution-implementation stage (as-is, to-be or as-built)
- description of design-content and decisions, in terms of a standardised architecture checklist
- list of known architectural issues (if any)

The checklist would be a simplified version of that used in the equivalent *Architecture Compliance Statement*.

Architecture Position Statement

An Architecture Position Statement may be created by enterprise- or domain-architects in Phase G, as a response to architecture-compliance reviews; or in hands-off architecture, as a response to one or more *Architecture Description Statements*. Its aim is to provide guidance for programme managers and other governance bodies, and describes recommended methods or actions to resolve architectural non-conformances in solution-designs or solution-implementations.

It is referenced in Phases G and H by designers and developers, architects, programme-managers, sponsor and other requestors for architecture services, and by stakeholder-'owners' of items in scope for the architecture cycle, governance bodies; and other stakeholders.

Typical content should include:

- identifiers for project, responsible persons and solution-implementation stage
- applicable *Architecture Compliance Statement* or *Architecture Description Statement* included by reference
- list of issues and recommended solutions

Architecture Dispensation Statement

The Architecture Dispensation Statement is prepared by an architect, to provides guidance for programme-management and longer-term governance of overall architecture. It identifies reasons to permit architectural non-conformance in a solution-design or solution-implementation, describes constraints applying to such permission, and recommends methods or actions to resolve such non-conformance in future.

It may be created in Phase D, as part of requirements for Phase E; in Phase E, as a response to solution-design constraints; in Phase F, as a response to project- or programme-sequence constraints; or in Phase G, in response to architecture-compliance reviews. It may be amended during Phases E-H. It is typically referenced by system designers and developers during Phases E-G, and by architects and others in reviews during any Phase.

Typical content should include:

- identifiers for project, responsible persons and solution-implementation stage
- applicable *Architecture Compliance Statement* included by reference
- reason to permit non-conformance (i.e. the 'dispensation')
- limits and constraints for dispensation – e.g. time-limit, scope-limit, etc
- description of recommended future path to architecture compliance

Phase completion reports – stakeholder reviews

The Phase Completion Report at the end of each of Phases B to G presents a staged status-review of work-to-date in the architecture cycle, and records the formal authority to proceed to the next Phase. (The initial *Statement of Architecture Work* provides the same function at the end of Phase A; likewise the *Architecture Charter* for the preliminary Phase P.)

Each report should be created by the lead-architect and others as appropriate, such as solution designers, programme- and project-managers, and optionally, the sponsor or delegate. It is mainly intended for use in the end-of-cycle review in Phase H, but reviews for all Phases may be referenced by architects, sponsors and other requestors; and the stakeholders and 'owners' of items in scope for the architectural cycle. Reviews for Phases E to G may also be referenced by system designers and developers, programme management body and other governance bodies, and other stakeholders.

Typical content for all Phases should include or reference:

- *Statement of Architecture Work* – usually included by reference
- summary of other items or information carried forward to other phases of this architectural cycle
- summary of requirements, issues and risks added to the respective repositories and/or registers
- summary of previous actions addressed and/or resolved during this phase
- summary of actions arising from the review-meeting

Context-specific content for Phase B should include or reference:

- baseline architecture (models, Architectural Building Blocks [ABBs], Solution Building Blocks [SBBs] etc in scope, as available at start of assessment)
- current-context architecture (models, ABBs, SBBs etc in scope, as available at end of assessment) – i.e. summary of results of this phase

Context-specific content for Phase C should include or reference:

- baseline architecture (models, ABBs, SBBs etc in scope for specified time-horizon(s), as available at start of assessment)
- future-context architecture(s) (models, ABBs, SBBs etc in scope for specified time-horizon(s), as available at end of assessment) – i.e. summary of results of this phase

Context-specific content for Phase D should include or reference:

- current-context architecture (models, ABBs, SBBs etc in scope, as available at end of Phase B assessment)
- future-context architecture(s) (models, ABBs, SBBs etc in scope for specified time-horizon(s), as available at end of Phase C assessment)

- gap-analysis assessment – i.e. summary of work conducted for this phase
- change-requirements for solutions and/or migration-plans – i.e. summary of results of this phase

Context-specific content for Phase E should include or reference:

- summary of solution-designs architectural assessment – i.e. summary of work conducted for this phase
- change-requirements for project- or migration-plans – i.e. summary of results of this phase

Context-specific content for Phase F should include or reference:

- summary of project-/migration-plan architectural assessment – i.e. summary of work conducted for this phase
- architectural-impact analysis of migration-plans – i.e. summary of results of this phase

Context-specific content for Phase G should include or reference:

- summary of project-implementation architectural assessment – i.e. summary of work conducted for this phase
- architectural-impact analysis of project-implementation – i.e. summary of results of this phase

Repositories

Architecture-models repository

The models repository (or 'Enterprise Continuum', in TOGAF terms) is a structured catalogue and storage for architecture models and other information. It is created in the Preliminary Phase, and referenced and updated by architects, business-analysts and others in all Phases – primarily Phase B and C – under governance as specified in the *Architecture Charter* and *Architecture Governance* documents.

Typical content should include:

- lists of 'primitives' (individual items)
- lists of structured relationships between primitives as model-type definitions
- instances of structured models or 'composites'
- sets of defined views or viewpoints into these primitives, relationships and composites; and
- formal definitions (metamodels) for the structures of each.

Re-usable items may also may be referred to as Architectural Building Blocks (of primitives) or Solution Building Blocks (of composites).

The repository should usually also contain standard reference-architectures for the organisation and the industry, and patterns of best-practice (the TOGAF 'Architecture Continuum' and 'Solutions Continuum' respectively).

Technical standards, industry standards, applicable legislation and other standards should be included by reference (the 'Standards Information Base', in the TOGAF specification).

In principle, the repository could consist solely of paper documents in a filing cabinet, or drawings in electronic form such as Visio diagrams, but ideally most or all of the content should be maintained within the data-structure of a purpose-built EA toolset. Dependent on the capabilities of the EA toolset, models may also be delivered in text-based report format.

Requirements repository

The requirements repository is a structured catalogue and storage for business-requirements, constraints, business-rules, business decisions such as strategies, policies and applicable regulations; and relationships between these items, such as 'implements', 'extends', 'conflicts with', etc. It should include requirements of any scope, from organisation-wide mandates (such as standards, legislation and the like) to project- or context-specific details.

In principle the repository could consist of paper documents in a filing cabinet, or simple project-specific registers in electronic form such as Excel spreadsheets, but ideally should be maintained as an enterprise-wide shared resource within the data-structure of a purpose-built requirements-management toolset, or preferably within the EA toolset that maintains the architecture repository.

If not already existing, the repository structure is defined and implemented during the Preliminary Phase, with governance specified in the Architecture Charter or Architecture Governance documents. It is updated by architects primarily in Phase D, and will be referenced and, where appropriate, updated by business analysts, developers and other stakeholders during any Phase.

Issues register and risks register

The issues register is a structured catalogue and storage for identified system-problems, change-requests, opportunities and other general issues; the persons assigned to address those issues;

and the status of each issue. It includes relationships between items, such as ' ‹amplifies›', '‹extends›', '‹resolves›', etc.

The risks register is a similar record-structure for identified business risks; the potential impact of each risk; the persons assigned to address each risk; the recommended means to mitigate such risks; and the status of each risk. It includes relationships between items, such as '‹amplifies›', '‹extends›', '‹impacts›', etc.

The registers include issues and risks of any scope, from project- or context-specific to organisation-wide. If not already existing, the registers should be created by the architecture lead during the Preliminary Phase, as authorised by a higher-level governance body. They are referenced and, in some cases, updated in all Phases by governance bodies, executive, architects, developers, process analysts, business analysts, developers, and other stakeholders as appropriate.

In principle the registers could consist of paper documents in a filing cabinet, or simple project-specific files in electronic form such as Excel spreadsheets, but ideally should be maintained as an enterprise-wide shared resource within the data-structure of a purpose-built issues-management toolset, preferably within the EA toolset.

Dispensations register

The dispensations register is a structured catalogue and storage for architectural dispensations; the potential impact of each dispensation; the validity and review-period for each dispensation; the persons assigned to address each dispensation; the recommended means to mitigate business risks implied by each dispensation; the actions taken to resolve each dispensation; and the status of each dispensation. The register may include relationships between items, such as '‹amplifies›', '‹extends›', '‹impacts›', etc.

The register includes dispensations applying at any level, from organisation-wide to project- or context-specific. It is created in the Preliminary Phase; updated primarily in Phase F or G, though occasionally in other Phases; and may be referenced in all Phases.

In principle the register could consist of paper documents in a filing cabinet, or simple project-specific files in electronic form such as Excel spreadsheets, but ideally should be maintained as an enterprise-wide shared resource within the data-structure of a purpose-built dispensations-management system, preferably as part of the EA toolset.

Glossary and Thesaurus

The glossary maintains formal agreed definitions for business and architectural terms. The thesaurus extends the glossary by identifying defined relationships between the glossary terms, such as:

- *'use'*: indicates that the term is a preferred meaning, alias or synonym of a term
- *'use for'*: indicates that the term is a non-preferred, deprecated or discontinued synonym, alias or meaning of another term (use the indicated 'use' version instead)
- *'broader term'*: indicates that the term has a wider meaning than the 'use' term to which it relates
- *'narrower term'*: indicates that the term has a narrower, more specific meaning than the 'use' term to which it relates
- *'related term'*: indicates that the term is generally associated with the concept of the related 'use' term, but is neither a synonym nor a broader or narrower term

In some cases – as in a 'jargon buster' tool – a thesaurus might also include alternate meanings or cross-references to *unrelated* terms. These would be references to items which might appear to be related, but are actually different, with different meanings from different contexts: a formal standard, or a descriptor for a business unit, or a software application, all with the same or similar term. For example, the acronym 'ISO' might represent 'Internal Service Order' as well as 'International Standards Organisation'.

Both glossary and thesaurus should be accessible in published form across the whole of the enterprise, such as via an intranet or extranet. If not already existing, they should be created in the Preliminary Phase. In the architecture cycle, they are updated primarily in Phase H, though occasionally in other Phases, and are referenced in all Phases.

Application

- What specifications exist in your current methodology for documents and other artefacts? What parts of each 'product' are mandated by the methodology? Which parts are optional, or for information only?
- What are the governance roles – if any – of each artefact? What part does each play in guiding and governing the methodology itself?

- What governance roles apply to each artefact? Who creates the artefact? Who signs it off? Who is responsible for review, for version-management and so on?
- What governance applies to the toolsets used to create, maintain and distribute each type of artefact? What version-management, archiving, migration to new host-systems, and suchlike?
- In what ways will these need to change as you expand the architecture to a full enterprise-wide scope?

Resources

TOGAF architecture products: see www.opengroup.org/architecture/togaf8-doc/arch/toc.html (chapter 'ADM Input and Output Descriptions')

COMPLETION – CLOSING THE LOOP

Summary

No matter how good the architecture development, it will only have real value for the enterprise if it is applied and put to practical use. The key requirement for this integration is some form of feedback and engagement of stakeholders, not only in the initial development of architecture, but also in its dissemination, review and re-use.

Details

Linking everything together

If architecture links everything together, how do we verify and measure that 'togetherness'? And how do we measure it in terms that are meaningful to the rest of the business? – because that's our real measure of success.

Enterprise-architecture maturity-models will help in this, up to a point. Most of the existing maturity-models are still either entirely IT-centric (such as that in TOGAF), or mostly so (such as the DyA and Meta Group models), so we need to adjust their scope somewhat to fit better with the scale and needs of whole-of-enterprise architecture. The Tetradian SEMPER metric may also be useful to gain a better sense of the impact and integration of the *human* side of enterprise systems, which rarely rate any kind of mention in IT-centric maturity-models.

As part of the end-of-cycle reviews – see 'Phase H – review lessons-learned' in *Methodology – solutions*, p.157 – you should always aim to identify, and, if possible, measure the enterprise-benefits gained as a result of any architecture work. This is not only to your own advantage – because you'll need to show that your work is achieving *something* useful! – but again also helps to link the enterprise together, by demonstrating the value for every-one of a whole-of-enterprise view.

It's essential, too, to ensure that benefits-metrics are assessed from a whole-of-enterprise perspective. Short-term financial 'return-on-investment', for example, is the kind of metric that most managers know and understand, but it can easily kill the company: Michael Porter describes the usual obsession with shareholder-value as "the Bermuda Triangle of strategy". Instead, we need to anchor the key metrics back to the core row-0 vision and values – and make sure that people understand *why* we need to do this.

> Two other books in this series, *Real Enterprise Architecture: beyond IT to the whole enterprise*, and *Power and Response-ability: the human side of systems*, go into this issue in more depth: you may find them useful in explaining its importance to business-managers and others.

A related area for architecture which is likely to be of real value to the enterprise is in searching for and resolving 'useless metrics', such as:

- reports compiled that no-one reads
- metrics which don't actually mean what they claim to mean
- metrics which present a subset of a whole issue as being the whole of the issue – such as measuring local efficiency without acknowledgement of impact on overall effectiveness
- quantitative measures used as the sole metrics for qualitative issues such as health and safety, ethics, responsibility, knowledge-sharing and quality itself

Resolving any of these issues is likely to require us to bridge across the silos – which means that we first need to have the formal authority to do so. Hence why we *need* the support of the CEO and the rest of executive before we set out to do this kind of work.

But note too that the aim here needs to be that of *bridging* the silos – not attempting to demolish them. Managers *like* silos: they give a sense of boundedness, of certainty in what is otherwise a very uncertain world. From an architecture perspective, and especially from an Agile perspective, silos make little sense, and are the undoubted source of many of our architectural problems: but they're a valuable operational convenience, and any attempt to dismantle them is likely to be regarded as a threat. Which will not help to improve the acceptance of enterprise architecture...

> In an architectural sense – certainly in the long term – silos are in effect a kind of organisational 'dispensation', and ought to be reviewed as such. But as a habit they're often so ingrained as 'the way we do things round here' that it can be quite difficult to get people to see that they *are* only a convenience, and that we could – and perhaps should – restructure them to suit a changing business world. One story we've found useful to illustrate this point goes as follows:

A young girl is learning how to cook. Her mother tells her that the Sunday joint *must* be cut in half before it's put in the oven. With a quizzical look, the girl asks why. "I don't know, darling", her mother replies, "but it's how your granny taught me, so I've always done it that way. Why don't you ask her?"

So the girl goes off to see grandmother, and asks the same question. "That's the way it *should* be done!" is the sharp response. "*Mother* did it that way, and you ought to know that a mother is *always* right!"

Still not convinced, but somewhat timidly, the girl approaches great-grandmother with the same question. "Oh no, dear", says the old woman, with a twinkle in her eye, "it's much better if it goes in the oven whole. But if you only have a small oven, like I do, you have to cut it in half to make it fit..."

Silos are just one organisational example of a response to constraints: there are many, many others. But whilst such constraints are real, they also change over time: so it's important to revisit and review on a regular basis whatever 'solutions' depend on those constraints. Paradoxically, one of the ways we link the enterprise together is by loosening the 'bindedness' to such constraints, to make it easier for the enterprise to move more freely, and respond to changes in its business environment in a more agile way.

Publish or perish?

In itself, enterprise architecture can provide a fascinating combination of intellectual challenge and emotional intensity. But it'll remain an 'academic exercise' unless we can take those ideas and put them to practical *use* – which is, after all, what the business is asking for. And the first part of that 'use' is simply letting people know what we're doing, and why.

In short, if we don't publish, we perish.

But publishing alone is not enough: we need to publish the right information, for the right purpose, to the right people, with all the right concerns around 'need to know, need to use'. Churning out 'shelfware' that no-one sees, let alone uses, is not exactly going to win us any friends: and we'll need all the help we can get if we're to extend the architecture to the whole of the enterprise.

Publishing the models and the like on an intranet or extranet is better than in bulky ring-binders – but not much better, if that's all we do. Before publishing *any* model, through *any* medium, we need to consider a whole range of extra issues that are not about architecture as such, but more about its *use* and *usability*:

- *Who are the audience for this model?* Different groups not only need different types of models, but may need different

186

presentations. Architects and designers are just about the only people who like the abstract 'boxes and lines' models so beloved by theorists: almost everyone else would much prefer a descriptive picture which shows what's going on in much more concrete terms. Executives need dashboards; front-line staff need clear quick-reference charts; neither groups have the designer's luxury of *time* to sit and think. Who are your audience? – keeping a model clean, clear and simple is not easy, but that's what they need from us.

- *How will they use this model?* In what ways will this model help them in their work? A model is both a description and a prediction about relationships – in this case, about some kind of entities or 'business objects' in a business context. What does each entity mean within the model? What is the model telling your audience, about relationships between those entities, about change, about action? We need to ensure that everything in the model makes practical sense, and can be put to practical use.

- *How will they find the right model?* Searching aimlessly through a shelf-full of unlabelled ring-binders is no-one's idea of fun, but trying to navigate our way through a badly-indexed intranet is no fun either. Hyperlinks make things even worse if we jump from one model to another but can't find our way back. Search-engines will help, but they can't do much unless we provide them with the right metadata with which to work. So these, together with careful thought on navigation-structure, and navigation-aids such as bookmarks, jump-lists and breadcrumb-trails, are all essential to help people put the architecture to use.

- *How will they know the model is current and correct?* One reason why shelfware remains on the shelf is because, even if people can find it, they don't know if it still applies. People can find information more easily on an intranet, but unless they *know* it's current and correct, they can't risk using it: they'll either have to hunt out the 'resident expert' – if there is one – or make a random guess – which increases the risk to the enterprise. To reduce that risk, every model not only needs to be easily accessible to the right people, but also needs clear, easily-interpreted metadata which describes its scope, its life-cycle and so on.

For large organisations especially, one area where even the most expensive of the EA toolsets start to earn their keep is in their publishing of models. Every toolset now can publish to an intranet; but

> some are definitely better than others in the way that they do it. Use those comments above as a checklist when you're reviewing the capabilities of different EA toolsets for your own enterprise.

The issue of lifecycle is another reason why architecture needs to be understood as a continuous process rather than the classic once-off 'fit and forget'. We *need* to promote a constant habit of 'refresh and re-use'. The world changes: but a printed model of that 'world' doesn't change itself to suit, and neither does a online model on an intranet unless we remember to update it. So one question we need to keep returning to in our Phase H reviews is whether there are any models that need to be updated. Triggers for such updates include:

- an entity in the model has changed status – for example, a physical server has been replaced (in an implementation-model), or an entire technology is reaching the 'sunset' stage of its lifecycle
- a related Reference Model has been changed – whether entities, relationships, or bindedness of either
- an existing Dispensation associated with the model, or with any item in model, has come up for review; or equally, a Dispensation has been applied to an item within the model

> Again, a good EA toolset can help in this, by auto-generating reports on any changes elsewhere that apply to entities, attributes or relationships within a chosen model or set of models. Another key item to add to that procurement-checklist.

Ideally, an update-review of any model should be treated as an entire architecture-cycle in its own right, all the way through from its own Phase A to Phase H. It's probably not viable in practice – if nothing else, the bureaucratic overhead would be enormous if applied to everything – but it's worthwhile keeping that ideal in mind as we work, and include reviews of appropriate existing models wherever practicable within all our architecture iterations.

Creating engagement

Engagement *is* the architecture: as architects we do provide the specialist skills and experience, perhaps, but getting people in general to think about all of their work in terms of architecture, of cross-enterprise impacts and the 'big picture', would have to be the real aim of what enterprise architecture is really all about. Engaging people in person, creating dialogue, garnering feedback, and *using* it, are all key parts in this process.

So how *do* we make this engagement happen?

The first part consists of acknowledging that it *is* essential. Which often isn't comfortable, because by the nature of the work, many of us tend to be "opinionated introverts" – hiding away in our own conceptual worlds, certain that we're right, and often not so skilled at dealing with other people and their opinions, especially when they diverge a long way from our own... It can seem somewhat of a personal challenge for us to face, but it's something that we do need to address within ourselves.

> There's a entire mini-industry, of course, that focuses on this one particular issue of interpersonal skills and communication in the business context. One of my favourite authors in this is the veteran 'consultant's consultant' from the IT industry, Gerry Weinberg. His classic *The Secrets of Consulting* is accurately described as "fun airplane reading for consultants", but it's also incisive and illuminating, and his storytelling and his brilliant use of 'one-liners' show how consulting can really work. The sequel, *More Secrets of Consulting*, is rather different, concentrating more on the personal skills and self-observation that the consultant will need, and how to develop them – and hence is perhaps a bit more challenging to read and apply in practice. But both books strongly recommended, anyway.

Another part consists of providing as much support as we can for that dialogue, so that it has a place and a context in which it *can* happen. Some of this needs to happen face-to-face: we need to be seen, to be known, to be recognised, and so on, if our words and images are to carry any weight at all. Once again, those interpersonal skills really *matter* here.

Increasingly, though, we also need to ensure that there's plenty of support for communication and conversation in the 'virtual world'. Some of this is for purely pragmatic reasons: face-to-face communication becomes impossibly expensive when your peers and stakeholders are scattered everywhere around the globe. But online tools also permit 'asynchronous' communication: reviewers can send their feedback at any time of day or night, and we can likewise respond at any time. Collaboration tools such as wikis – user-editable websites – and other business-oriented 'Enterprise 2.0' social software can all help in this: it's well worth experimenting to see which ones will work best in your own architecture environment.

> Chris Collison and Geoff Parcell's book *Learning To Fly* is one of many useful resources for this – it's not actually about flying, but about how they created conditions for enterprise-wide knowledge-sharing at BP, with a particular emphasis on online tools and online collaboration, and on the social tactics needed to get groups of hard-nosed engineers to share ideas and to feel safe enough to openly ask each other for help.

> And once again, the various EA toolsets differ widely in the feedback facilities that they provide. Whilst all will publish to an intranet, in many cases they still only provide a 'read-only' one-way trip – which does let people know what's going on, but doesn't provide any real support for that much-needed engagement. The better tools will allow users to add their own annotations and comments; the best will even permit users to amend the models themselves, all under full access-control. Whichever way you play it, get the best facilities in this that you can afford: it'll more than pay for itself in the long run.

And finally, what we really need to happen is for the enterprise to take on the 'ownership' of architecture itself. When that happens, we're able to drop back to a 'hands-off' style of architecture – see *Methodology – hands-off architecture*, p.161. But to get there, we need to create conditions under which the engagement in architecture exists not only between us and our stakeholders, but between all of the stakeholders as well.

At this point, architecture will need to intersect with other fields such as change management and knowledge management, to address issues that include:

- knowledge-sharing through 'communities of practice', such as described by Etienne Wenger and his colleagues
- narrative knowledge and 'business story-telling', such as described by Shawn Callahan and others at the Australian consultancy Anecdote
- developing and sustaining a proactive, self-adapting 'learning organisation', such as described by Peter Senge and colleagues

Engagement across the enterprise is what closes the loop for architecture. At that point, it becomes an ongoing 'virtuous cycle', continually expanding outward, extending the benefits of whole-of-enterprise integration and the whole-of-enterprise view.

And that's what the business really wants from us. That's what it's always wanted: IT-architecture was only ever an intermediate step towards that aim.

So you now have the tools and enough of the broader context to extend your IT-architecture skillset and experience to that greater goal. Hone them in further practice, and use them well!

Application

- What metrics are currently used to assess the *overall* business-value of enterprise-architecture?

- What metrics are currently used to measure the value of the enterprise itself? In what terms (or whose terms) are those metrics defined? To what extent – if at all – do they align with the espoused vision and values of the enterprise? If the alignment is poor, what could enterprise-architecture do to improve it?
- What processes and tools do you use to engage stakeholders in the various stages of the architecture process – particularly the review-phases?
- What support does your existing architecture-toolset provide in this? If any exists, is it unidirectional (broadcast only), annotation, or fully bidirectional?
- What 'need to know / need to use' access-control is required for this? How do you manage the appropriate security requirements and implementation?

Resources

- DyA Architecture Maturity Matrix: see
  eng.dya.info/Home/services/architecture_maturity_model.zip
- Martin van den Berg and Marlies van Steenbergen, *Building an Enterprise Architecture Practice: tools, tips, best practices, ready-to-use insights* (Sogeti / Springer Verlag, 2006)
- Meta Group Architecture Maturity Audit: *Meta Group Practice*, (2000), Vol 4 No.4 (for Part 1) and No.5 (for Part 2)
- SEMPER metric: see Tom Graves, *SEMPER and SCORE: enhancing enterprise effectiveness* (Tetradian, 2008)
- Background to SEMPER metric: see Tom Graves, *Power and Response-ability: the human side of systems* (Tetradian, 2008)
- Whole-of-enterprise architecture: see Tom Graves, *Real Enterprise Architecture: beyond IT to the whole enterprise* (Tetradian, 2008)
- Gerald M Weinberg, *The Secrets of Consulting: a guide to giving and getting advice successfully* (Dorset House, 1986)
- Gerald M Weinberg, *More Secrets of Consulting: the consultants toolkit* (Dorset House, 2002)
- Engagement in knowledge-sharing: see Chris Collison and Geoff Parcell, *Learning to Fly: practical lessons from one of the world's leading knowledge companies* (Capstone, 2001)
- Etienne Wenger on 'communities of practice': see
  www.ewenger.com/theory/

📖 Etienne Wenger, Richard McDermott and William M. Snyder, *Cultivating Communities of Practice: a guide to managing knowledge* (Harvard Business School Press, 2002)

🏛 Narrative knowledge and business-storytelling: see www.anecdote.com.au

📖 Peter Senge et al., *The Dance of Change: the challenges of sustaining momentum in learning organizations* (Nicholas Brealey Publishing, 1999)

GLOSSARY

This summarises some of the terms and acronyms we've come across in the book.

ADM acronym for Architecture Development Method, the methodology used in *TOGAF* to guide development of *enterprise architecture*

ArchiMate a visual language used to model *enterprise architectures*, developed by Netherlands consortium Telematics

ARIS acronym for Architecture of Integrated Systems, a production-oriented *enterprise architecture* framework developed by German group IDS-Scheer

chaos domain in the *Cynefin* model, domain of inherent uncertainty and unpredictability; decisions are guided by *principles* and *values*; represented in the business context by unique market-of-one customisation and by non-repeatable maintenance issues; also useful when deliberately invoked in creativity, in *narrative* and *dialogue*, and in *foresight* techniques such as *scenario* construction

complex domain in the *Cynefin* model, domain of *emergent* properties and non-linear relationships between factors; decisions are derived from heuristics and guidelines; unlike *chaos*, which is inherently uncertain, may often create an illusion of predictability, especially where linear analysis is applied within a short-term, narrow set of assumptions

Cynefin model of organisational *complexity* developed by David Snowden of Cognitive Edge, which describes four distinct *paradigms* to interpret a given context: *known*, *knowable*, *complex* and *chaotic*

DyA acronym for Dynamic Architecture, an *enterprise-architecture* framework developed by Netherlands consultancy Sogeti

effective 'on purpose', producing the intended overall result with an *optimised* balance over the whole; requires broad generalist awareness of the whole, rather than the narrow focus required to create local efficiency, hence often contrasted with *efficient*

efficient	'doing more with less', creating the maximum result with minimum use or wastage of resources in a specific activity or context; improved incrementally through *active learning* and related techniques for feedback and reflection, although major improvements usually require a change in *paradigm*; an *EREAI* theme associated with the *mental dimension* of the context
emergence	context within which cause-effect patterns can be identified only retrospectively, and in which analytic techniques are usually unreliable and misleading
enterprise architecture	a systematic process to model and guide *integration* and *optimisation* of the information-technology of an enterprise or (at higher maturity-levels) the entire enterprise
FEAF	acronym for Federal Enterprise Architecture Framework, a framework and methodology developed for *enterprise architecture* by the US government
goal	a specific objective to be achieved by a specified point in time; emphasis on the *physical* or *behavioural dimension* of *purpose*, contrasted with *mission*, *role* and *vision*
knowable domain	in the *Cynefin* model, domain of 'the complicated', with identifiable cause-effect relationships; decisions are derived from contextual analysis
known domain	in the *Cynefin* model, domain of certainty and known cause-effect relationships; decisions are predefined by laws, rules and regulations
mission	a desired capability or state to be achieved, usually within a specified timeframe, and to be maintained indefinitely once achieved; emphasis on the *emotional* and, to a lesser extent, the *mental dimensions* of *purpose*, contrasted with *goal*, *role* and *vision*
narrative	personalised and often emotive expression or interpretation of knowledge, as history, anecdote or story; link-theme between *mental dimension* and *emotional dimension*
optimisation	process of *integration* in which *efficiency* in different areas is traded-off and balanced for maximum *effectiveness* over the whole, between different layers and sub-contexts such as departments, business processes and business units
principle	a conceptual commitment or model, the *mental-dimension* equivalent of *value*

purpose	an expression of individual and/or collective identity - the *aspirational* theme of "who we are and what we stand for"; incorporates distinct dimensions of *vision, role, mission* and *goal*
recursion	patterns of relationship or interaction repeat or are 'self-similar' at different scales; permits simplification of otherwise complex processes
role	a declared focus or *strategic* position within the 'world' described by a *vision*; emphasis on the *conceptual* or *mental* and, to a lesser extent, the *emotional dimensions* of *purpose*, contrasted with *goal, mission* and *vision*
scenario	an imagined future context, developed for the purpose of understanding both the present context and options for action in the future context
strategy	'big picture' view of an action-plan for an organisation to implement a *purpose*, usually emphasizing its *vision, role* and *mission* components; contrasted with the *tactics* required to execute the plan
tactics	detailed *missions, goals* and other step-by-step activities to execute a *strategy*, or some segment of an overall strategy
TOGAF	acronym for The Open Group Architecture Framework, an IT-oriented framework and methodology for *enterprise architecture* developed collectively by members of the Open Group consortium
value	an emotional commitment, also associated with the *relational* domain
vision	description of a desired 'world', always far greater than any individual or organization; described in the present tense, yet is never 'achieved'; emphasis on the *aspirational dimension* of *purpose*, contrasted with *goal, mission* and *role*; also link-theme between *aspirational dimension* and *emotional dimension*
visioning	generic term for the process of identifying, developing and documenting *vision* and *values*, leading towards *strategy* and *tactics*
Zachman framework	a systematic structure for categorisation of models within an IT-oriented *enterprise architecture*, developed by John Zachman

Printed in the United Kingdom
by Lightning Source UK Ltd.
135489UK00001B/298-327/P

9 781906 681029